D1370185

JOYFUL FLUENCY

JOYFUL FLUENCY:

Brain-Compatible Second Language Acquisition

©1998 The Brain Store®

JOYFUL FLUENCY:
Brain-Compatible Second Language Acquisition

Lynn Freeman Dhority
with Eric Jensen

Editor: Karen Markowitz
Designer: Tracy Linares

All rights reserved. Written permission required
from the publisher to use or reproduce
any part of this book except for
brief quotations in critical reviews or articles.
Printed in Canada

*Additional copies may be ordered through the publisher listed below. Call, write or fax for
volume pricing. Checks, purchase orders and credit cards welcome.*

©**1998 The Brain Store**®
4202 Sorrento Valley Blvd. Suite B
San Diego, CA 92121
(858) 546-7555 phone
(858) 546-7560 fax
E-Mail: info@thebrainstore.com
www.thebrainstore.com

ISBN # 1-890460-01-X

*Dedicated to
teachers everywhere
who are ready
to share their joy...*

Preface

This book represents a compilation of ideas formed over a period of 25 years. My foundation for the exciting foreign language teaching career path I have followed began with my initial exposure in the 1970's to the ground-breaking work of Georgi Lozanov, a pioneer in the accelerated learning movement, wedded with my experience in psychosynthesis and other approaches to learning. What seemed like an effective, albeit experimental, educational approach at that time has now evolved into a proven approach to language acquisition informed by years of practical classroom application and research.

The brain-compatible language acquisition model presented in *Joyful Fluency* is representative of the brain power of many leading neurologists, physicists, systems theorists and educators who have, by virtue of their work, created a paradigm shift that is redefining the education process for the next century. This research-based multidisciplinary approach considers how we, as facilitators of learning, can become more "brain-friendly" or aware of the brain's role in teaching and learning.

The purpose of *Joyful Fluency* is to provide a practical guide for those who wish to learn how to use the brain-compatible acquisition model to enhance language teaching and learning. Informed by various human development theories and language acquisition models, The Joyful Fluency Model recognizes the valuable contributions of behaviorists, scientists and educators such as: Carl Jung, Roberto Assagioli, Roger Sperry, Paul MacLean, Howard Gardner, Leslie Hart, Sally Springer, Georg Deutsch, Georgi Lozanov, Stephen Krashen, James J. Asher, and Tracy Terrell (see bibliography for exact references).

We recommend you use this book in a way that is most natural for your brain to learn - that is, in both wholes and in parts, sequentially and randomly. For example, you might conduct an initial browsing over the contents and chapter headings, bookback and first chapter. Then read one chapter at a time. As you read through it, make notes. Try things out in your own classroom. Reflect on the process and dialogue with others. Important shifts in your teaching occur not from reading the material alone, but from trying it out. Work with the ideas, and play with them. Just as you'll be asking your students to do, we ask you to jump into the process, relax and have fun. Your learning is inevitable!

"*The discovery that human language learning was instinctual shattered the prevailing paradigm. Until that time, everyone, from mothers to second language teachers believed they were actually teaching the target language. In reality, they were merely orchestrating the conditions for a natural, rather automatic acquisition. It is a mind-boggling realization that humans are designed to learn complex languages effortlessly. The reality is, therefore, that language fluency ought to be a joyful process*"

Eric Jensen, *The Learning Brain*

Table of Contents

Introduction

In schools everywhere, teachers and students are influenced by the emotion of fear. The very process of education, which is after all one of growth and change, is itself an anxiety producer. Many of our most strongly held convictions are formed around core fears established very early in our lives. When these are challenged, we might think our safety is threatened. As a result, we often create an impenetrable shell around our belief systems and guard vigilantly against any cracks in it. This response, however, may bind us to behavior patterns that no longer serve us. Since our belief system has a determining influence on how we teach and learn, we must continue to redefine and refine it as the world around us evolves. As teachers, our ability to meet the challenges of the day is dependent upon how well we learn, change and grow. My own classroom experience provides potent testimony to this.

Many years ago when I was fresh out of graduate school I taught language classes in the conventional way - using the audio-lingual approach in vogue at that time. I did not know any better. I simply followed the model of my own teachers. I was anxious to succeed, afraid of appearing incompetent and, perhaps, too inexperienced to challenge the basic assumptions underlying the standard methodology. I was an energetic, committed teacher and taskmaster. My prevailing attitude was work hard, sacrifice much, and the rewards will eventually follow. This approach was representative of the belief system that language learning requires a great deal of drudgery and drilling. I introduced dialogues, exercises and grammar presentations from the textbook; then tested, graded, and drilled all the harder. My classes were intense and demanding, and some students who could withstand the pace "learned" a lot. This was not, however, a classroom that I can describe as joyful. And I can't help but wonder how many of my original students are speaking German today?

As a new teacher, I was skeptical of alternative approaches which promised language learning without the struggle and stress I had endured. I was supposed to have learned the *right* way to teach in college. Could a better method really be possible? Then, my exposure to Georgi Lozanov's model of accelerated learning in the 1970's convinced me that my own fear of change was the dragon I had to slay. As I practiced embracing the unknown, my playful, intuitive and spontaneous self emerged more freely. At the same time, similar changes occurred in my students. As I modeled risk-taking in my teaching, I invited imaginative, playful communication in my classroom. Once the first risky steps were taken safely, a flow of positive energy provided the needed momentum for maximum learning to take place.

Now, many years later, my teaching bears little resemblance to its rough beginnings. Thanks to some wonderful teacher-guides, my teaching style has moved beyond the veneer of institutional authority. From the description of my early teaching style, it is probably obvious that I did not dare "play" in class. The thought of bringing a hand puppet into a college or adult-education class (as I now do regularly) would have been dismissed without consideration. I would have felt self-conscious, afraid of insulting adult students or of looking foolish. My teaching style is now a way of life which includes a healthy diet of risk-taking, creative experimentation, playful classroom behavior and a great deal of joy. My experience supports the premise that "who we are"- the beliefs and attitudes with which we identify - is inextricably intertwined with how we teach. We suggest, influence and communicate in a myriad of ways with our students. Our students, in turn, begin to reflect back to us the images we project. Though we would all love to have a "magic pill" in the medicine cabinet of learning, we know that the only magic that exists is within us.

Most of us have grappled with the strain of shifting perspectives and the introduction of new paradigms. Acknowledging our beliefs is the starting point. Once we accept that apprehension is part of the change process, perhaps, we won't be as likely to shy away from it. From my own evolutionary process of becoming a successful teacher, I realize now that it was I who was the limiting influence on my student's learning, not them. If I wanted to get better results in my language classes, I needed to find tools that were more effective, to embody the same qualities that I wanted my students to mirror; and to demonstrate the willingness to risk fully, engage wholeheartedly and experience enthusiastically the joy that can be derived from learning.

In the following pages, I invite you to hold to the thought of being the best educator you can possibly be, to view realistically your current belief system, to face the fears of implementing new paradigms; and ultimately to become the risk-taking, joyful learner that you wish for your students.

Lynn Freeman Dhority
November, 1997

Chapter 1
Language Learning and the Human Brain: Key Principles

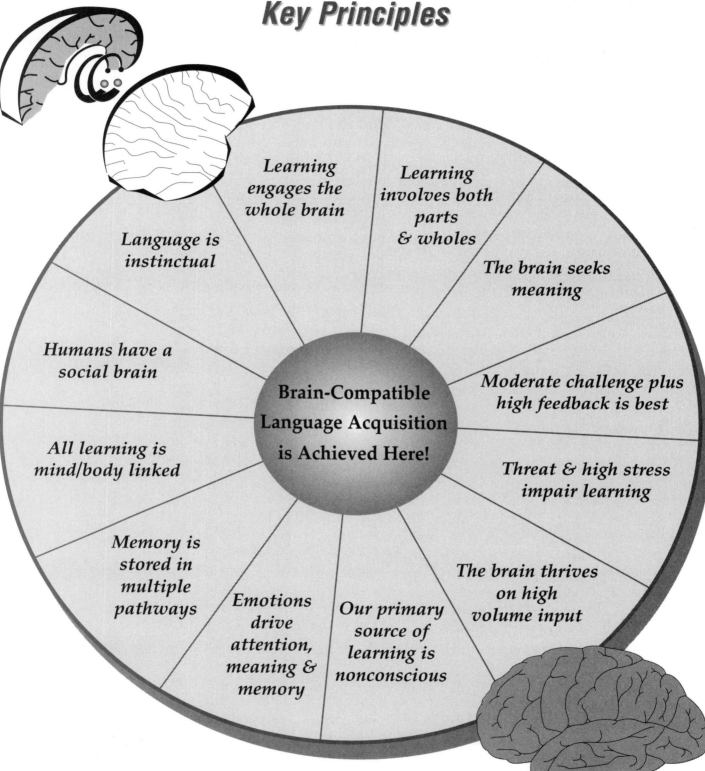

Learning engages the whole brain

Learning involves both parts & wholes

The brain seeks meaning

Language is instinctual

Humans have a social brain

Moderate challenge plus high feedback is best

All learning is mind/body linked

Brain-Compatible Language Acquisition is Achieved Here!

Threat & high stress impair learning

Memory is stored in multiple pathways

The brain thrives on high volume input

Emotions drive attention, meaning & memory

Our primary source of learning is nonconscious

Language Learning And The Human Brain

Background

Can learning a new language really be joyful and exciting? The premise of this book is that, *yes*, it can be. Though many of us probably have not had this experience, we are tuned into the possibility of it. An explosion of research in neuroscience and related fields is informing educators worldwide as to how the brain naturally learns best. Based on these brain-compatible principles, foreign language learning is finding a powerful new identity, one that is aligned with the leading edge research; and is, therefore, more learner-friendly. The purpose of *Joyful Fluency* is to inspire maximum learning in an environment informed by this emerging paradigm. Though encompassing in scope and magnitude, the principles of brain-compatible language acquisition are not difficult to implement, nor beyond the grasp of every teacher. Foreign language learning today has the possibility of being your student's favorite subject.

The paradox of language learning is that it is both a highly complex process and simple enough for a child to learn. In the traditional public school setting over the last few decades, many students learned fragments of a foreign language - enough to feel comfortable, perhaps, with the basic salutations. However, few students achieved competency in a non-native language, and even fewer became bilingual. Though foreign language classes have been required in United States public schools for decades, typically these courses aren't offered until middle or high school. Unfortunately, the failure rate is high. All of us have either heard stories or had experiences with language classes that weren't very positive. At best, they produced high anxiety. At worst, they were humiliating. Other countries are succeeding at second language acquisition, why aren't we? The purpose of this chapter is to provide a backdrop for understanding a dynamic model of language acquisition that proposes to reverse this high failure rate. This brain-compatible model is known as Joyful Fluency (JoF).

The brain-compatible approach to learning a new language maintains that high anxiety and humiliation are not only unnecessary, they are detrimental. Though it is true that *some* stress accompanies most new learning, you will soon see how brain-compatible principles maximize achievement. In a climate of enjoyment, learning is naturally accelerated. The win-win in this paradigm-shift is that students *and* teachers enjoy the rewards - increased participation, deeper understanding, greater confidence, a boost in motivation, fewer discipline problems, less unproductive time, decreased stress levels and lasting results. Benefits like these are why brain-compatible learning has achieved the magnitude of a learning revolution.

From Inkwells to the World Wide Web

Education has advanced radically in the twentieth century. Such dramatic change has taken place that the schoolmarm and schoolroom of yesteryear are as unrecognizable today as the eccentric diagnoses and cures of physicians popular at the turn of the last century. Now, teachers who inflict corporal punishment for incomplete homework or rap knuckles for poor penmanship are as outdated, fortunately, as doctors who treat headaches with neck leeches or blame mental illness on evil spirits. The incredible technological advances that characterize modern medical centers and our educational institutions, have left in their wake the absurdity of these bygone beliefs. We are replacing these beliefs with an educational model that now rests squarely on science.

Through the use of positron emission tomography (PET) and magnetic resonance imaging (MRI), researchers are currently forming a biological picture of how the brain operates - an electronic map, so-to-speak, of the functional human cerebral cortex. Electroencephalograms (EEG) use computerized electrodes to detect various brain states and provide readings about the electrical output of the brain, helping us track, for example, how much activity is going on while problem-solving. The determinations we can make from these and other technological advances provide us with a biologically-based view of the brain in learning. Teaching and learning in a way that is compatible with what we now know about the brain is the basis for this book. In fact, this research-based paradigm-shift is influencing the full scope of teaching practices from assessment, physical environments, and curriculum to instructional strategies, discipline approaches and organizational structures.

Beyond the value of a biologically-based pedagogy, the techno-tools available to the current generation of learners makes teaching and learning more accessible, exciting and relevant than ever before. Computers that are networked to classrooms around the globe with a central "brain" like the World Wide Web engage learners in real-life learning never imagined in decades past. Though, the amount of information our brains are required to synthesize in this technological era is truly mind-boggling, teachers everywhere are rising to meet the challenge.

Though, the amount of information our brains are required to synthesize in this technological era is truly mind-boggling, teachers everywhere are rising to meet the challenge

From Brain-Compatible Learning to Language Acquisition

The brain-compatible language acquisition model detailed in *Joyful Fluency* is informed by both research on the brain and psycholinguistics. The critical influences that contribute to these combined approaches are explored in-depth in chapter two. Their shared cornerstone, however, is what noted linguist Steven Pinker calls the language instinct. Human language development is as natural as learning to eat. With this emphasis in mind, language learning can become a joyful and natural experience.

Teaching in a way that is not brain-compatible is like a doctor performing surgery in a non-sterile environment; it is foolhardy and detrimental. Some of the key premises that distinguish brain-compatible learning are: • Each brain is unique • High stress and threat impair learning • Learning is influenced by specific developmental stages or "windows" of opportunity • The brain can grow new connections at any age • Emotions are critical to learning • Information is stored in multiple memory pathways • The mind-body connection in learning is inseparable • Patterns drive understanding • The brain thrives on meaning • Much learning is subconscious • The brain develops better in concert with others • The brain adapts to its environment based on its unique experience.

In an enriched environment where infants hear a great deal of conversation, language skills flourish

From Conception to Five Years

Though the brain is a work in progress, childhood experiences influence its circuitry which will form the "perceptual map" of the individual. By six months of age, reports Dr. Patricia Kuhl of the University of Washington, infants in English-speaking homes already have different auditory maps (as shown by electrical measurements that identify which neurons respond to different sounds) from those in Swedish-speaking homes (Begley, 1996). Theoretically, a new language can be learned at any age; however, it has been determined that stages of developmental readiness or specific windows for optimal acquisition exist which if not engaged at the appropriate time can be more difficult to access later on. Though there is some controversy as to when the specific developmental windows are open for language learning, it is generally accepted that the first five years are essential. Certainly, in the first 24 months, language fluency can be enhanced or impaired by intervention.

At the prenatal stage, environmental factors are already influencing the embryo's brain. Toxins such as tobacco smoke, alcohol, and drugs, as well as high stress, negatively impact the developing embryo. Studies suggest that deficits in these areas specifically impair language learning. Physiological factors such as inner ear infections in early childhood have also been shown to impair language development. On the other hand, in an enriched environment where infants hear a great deal of conversation, language skills flourish. "Parentese", the common parenting talk which is heavily accentuated and spoken slowly and repetitively to infants, is believed to be less important than earlier thought. However, infants whose parents talk to them more frequently and use bigger "adult" words will develop better language skills, reports Dr. Peter Huttenlocher at the University of Chicago (Begley, 1996).

At birth, the human brain emerges from the womb with over 100 billion cells intact. Prepared for a world of countless language possibilities, the infant brain is gifted with more than a trillion total pre-existing synaptic connections. Synapses are the junctions between two brain cells. At this time, circuits in the auditory cortex are allocating both cells and receptor sites for what is deemed the early survival sounds of the native language. Infants quickly develop, in their first year, a perceptual map of responsive neurons in the auditory cortex. This talking and hearing map is formed by hearing distinguishable sounds, accents and word pronunciations. These phonemes alert infants to the particular inflections of the native language like a Spanish rolled "r" or a Japanese sharp "hi"! As a result, the brain dedicates special neurons to be receptive to those particular sounds. Children are soon ready for a flood of longer words if you attach the activity to the word and imbue it with inflection, tempo, volume and body language. Remarkably, by age two, most infants know 1,000 words.

During the first couple years of life, there is a huge vocabulary to be acquired. By age one, infants have heard most of the verbal sounds of their native language and have learned to distinguish the native dialect including accent, tempo, and rhythm. Language sounds that have not been heard by the infant and processed in the brain by this age, are not likely to be acquired later without a non-native pronunciation. Kuhl says "By 12 months, infants have lost the ability to discriminate sounds that are not significant in their language" (Begley, 1996). By this time, the basis for the brain's auditory map which lays the foundation for speaking has been set. This developing map is so customized for the household that the infant is raised in, that children are "functionally deaf" to sounds outside of their home environments.

How can language learning be impaired at this age? A lack of parental stimulation is one way. Parents need to read to their children, talk to them and allow them to make mistakes. That's where television falls short, reports Huttenlocher. "Language development has to be used in relation to ongoing events, or it's just noise," he says (Begley, 1996). That incoherent noise does *not* build new connections in the brain. There is no evidence at this time that listening to television can build language skills in infants. By age three, most infants are fluent and grammar is used to form sentences. The greater the early vocabulary children are exposed to, the better. In the midst of this early language acquisition period, an intense neural competition for space rewards mobilized synapses with survival and eliminates static ones. Thus, for the first ten years of a child's life, the brain is busy pruning away excess connections. This pruning shapes the ability of all of us to learn languages. The old adage "use it or lose it" sums up the effect of this early pruning process.

Optimal Time For Second Language Learning

Many researchers, including Dr. Elizabeth Bates of the Center for Research on Language and Cognition at the University of California, San Diego, say that the optimal time for learning a second language is from age five to ten years. This is due to the fact that by this age the brain has already learned the structure, syntax and vocabulary of one language. The ability to communicate is already in place; yet the brain still has new language acquisition architecture intact, as well. There are countless neurons and synapses that have not yet been pruned away. Research suggests that all elementary schools should insure children are exposed to at least one second language during this critical window of opportunity.

What about learning language at age ten years and older? How important is early language exposure? Widely publicized case studies of children who have survived in isolation from humans and are discovered after the age of ten report that these children never learned to talk. The brain has simply pruned away or reallocated the neural structures needed for coherent human speech. By this age we've also lost the ability to pick up and activate the native accent in the same way that a younger child would be able to. Fortunately, most children are exposed to their native language and learn to speak effortlessly even in less than adequate physical and emotional environments. However, certainly, high stress during the first ten years of a child's life can trigger the brain's functional priority for survival at the expense of developing higher-order thinking skills. Responding to this optimal window for language acquisition, more and more school districts are implementing bilingual immersion programs and second language exposure in the early elementary grades.

Adult Language Learning

Typically, learning certain languages can provide a template for learning related others. For example, Spanish speakers will likely find it easier to learn Italian and Portuguese. And if you learn Danish, you'll be able to learn Swedish and Norwegian much easier. Research tells us that the brain continues to "re-wire" itself with the production of synapses throughout our life. The more we learn, the more we physically change our brain. For decades it was thought that the brain did not generate new cells. The newest research, however, suggests that the brain, in fact, does grow new cells with proper stimulation (at least in the hippocampus, an area responsible for memory). This means there is still significant potential for adults without any early childhood exposure to acquire a foreign language. This may not be easy to believe since the record of success in American schools suggests otherwise. Over 95 percent of adults with a college education have taken a second language course; and yet, less than 5 percent of them are comfortable using it.

Learning certain languages can provide a template for learning related others

5

As an adolescent or adult, language learning is influenced by different developmental boundaries. Much neural pruning has taken place. However, the good news is that, as a general rule, the brain is more "plastic" than fixed. An adult's independence can provide the potential for rich opportunities usually not available to a child. It should not be discounted that adult motivations and a more expansive life experience can provide a sufficient foundation for second language learning. In fact, certain Indian tribes in the Amazon basin are well known for speaking over a dozen languages; and most of these languages are acquired in adulthood (Krashen in Blair, p. 28).

The success potential for learning a second language as an adult can be increased dramatically by visiting the culture in which the language is spoken. Associations, vocabulary and context necessary for fluency are increased tenfold by immersion within that culture. The Amazon tribes simply listen to other languages until they feel comfortable enough to speak them. Another option for adult learners is called orchestrated immersion. This powerful learning approach is generated when language is taught in a coherent, rich, multi-sensory language "bath" by an instructor aware of the brain-compatible methodologies possible. This is much like the immersion saturation found in another country, but the instructor must orchestrate the process. This is the basis for the brain-compatible language acquisition model presented in *Joyful Fluency*.

Reader's Reflection

What was your own experience of learning a second language like?

Key Principles of Language Learning and the Brain

As teachers or facilitators of learning, we ought to understand the brain's key operating principles and use them as guidelines. By itself, one principle is not likely to transform your teaching or training. But taken as an aggregate, and implemented over time, you can expect significant positive results. The following 12 brain-compatible principles are most relevant to language acquisition:

1 *Language Learning Engages the Whole Brain*

Neuroscientists and reductionists in particular are, of course, very interested in localization of brain activity. In the 1970's the left/right brain theory was popularized which supported a neat separation of mental functions to either of the hemispheres. This overly-simplistic theory resulted in an inaccurate public perception of the brain as having dichotomous functional areas when, in fact, the brain is a bilateral organ that operates interdependently. But as educators, the location of brain function is far less important than the functions themselves. Even the colorful, well-publicized computer-generated scans of brain activity show only the most highly contrasting brain events. Much activity on the opposite hemisphere would not show up simply because the experiment may have not been sensitized to or "benchmarked" for a lower level of blood flow. Researchers have discovered that patients who had damage in one area of their brain used for language, shifted language production to another area of the brain. In short, we must acknowledge the integration of the brain before we talk about the modularity of it. Figure 1-A portrays a top view of the brain showing the divisions of left and right brain hemispheres.

The brain is a bilateral organ that operates inter-dependently

Figure 1-A

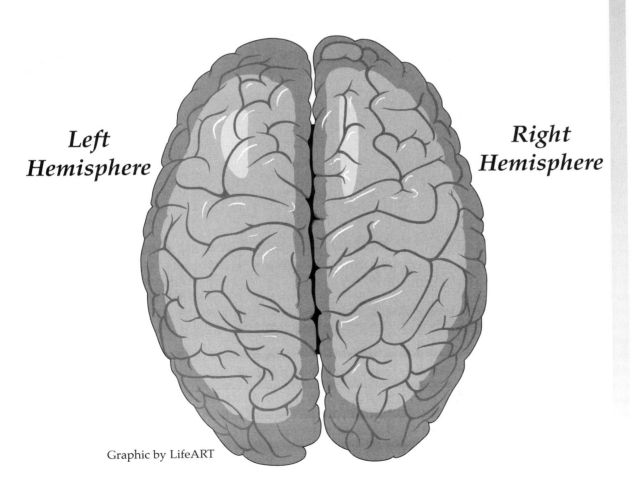

Left Hemisphere

Right Hemisphere

Graphic by LifeART

Language Learning Involves Processing Both Parts and Wholes

While early research focused on the left hemisphere dominance in the process of language learning, a more updated and appropriate model is one of complex, simultaneous input followed by the processes of analysis and synthesis. In fact, early language development seems to be remarkably bi-hemispheric. This makes sense because the rapidly growing body of brain research suggests that most brain functions overlap. Since both hemispheres are interconnected, it is unwise to speak simplistically of left-brain or right-brain methods.

If we agree that we want the qualities of both hemispheres to infuse the educational process, it would be wiser to talk less of hemispheric location and concentrate on creating balanced, inclusive, and comprehensive educational experiences. Sally Springer and Georg Deutsch, in their well-respected book, *Left Brain, Right Brain*, document dozens of anatomical and functional differences to each hemisphere. But they caution against reigniting the left/right brain debate. They argue that the brain is designed to work as an integrated system. Though the following dichotomies represent the original attributes of the left/right brain theory, they are still used symbolically as general indicators of corpus collassum functioning:

The rapidly growing body of brain research suggests that most brain functions overlap

Left Hemisphere:	Right Hemisphere:
Convergent	Divergent
Intellectual	Intuitive
Deductive	Inductive
Rational	Imaginative
Obvious	Metaphorical
Abstract	Concrete
Realistic	Impulsive
Directed	Free Choice
Sequential	Random
Historical	Timeless
Analytical	Non-judgmental
Explicit	Implicit
Objective	Subjective
Successive	Simultaneous

The Brain is a Natural Meaning-Maker

The human brain is a natural meaning-seeker and meaning-maker. The variables responsible for this creation of personal meaning are correlated, but not causal. They include the importance of personal relevance, the engagement of emotion and the elicitation and formation of complex pattern-making in context. Unless a concerted effort is made by a facilitator to ensure that these elements are included in the curriculum, acquisition will be slow. What occurs in the brain at the moment of meaning-making is far from clear. This principle reminds us that language learning must be coherent, relevant and meaningful to maximize the process. Learning vocabulary words, for example, out of context makes little sense. Real situations and simulations do, however, make sense. What is clear is that learning without meaning is unlikely to be recalled, used or enjoyed.

The Brain Learns Best with Moderate Challenge and High Feedback

In both animal and human studies, optimal brain growth (and presumably, learning) took place in a moderately challenging environment with high levels of feedback. Such an environment is probably much like the one in which you, as an infant, learned your native tongue. You probably heard many people around you speaking the language and you likely received constant feedback on your own speaking efforts.

Unfortunately, in traditional second language classes, the primary instructional methodology is a teacher or trainer doing most of the talking. This action is in direct contrast to the strong base of neurological evidence that suggests interactive, challenging enriched environments are far better for learning. Learners need wide ranging levels of feedback, they need control over the feedback, and they need the instructor to be a minor part of that feedback equation. The specifics of making this happen are detailed in later chapters.

Learning without meaning is unlikely to be recalled, used, or enjoyed

Reader's Reflection

In what ways do you make certain your students receive wide-ranging feedback?

Threat and High Stress Impair Learning

It is commonly known that what is experienced as threat or high stress to one person may be considered petty annoyance to another. Nonetheless, each of us knows what it is like to feel threatened or stressed. Both experiences change the body's chemistry and impair learning. The brain's response to fear is a shifting of its priorities resulting in more simplistic and inhibited patterns. Commonly, the brain's peripheral learning is, therefore, reduced as is attraction to novelty and some types of memory.

Risk-taking is a critical ingredient to the process of second language learning; and classrooms or social conditions that don't feel safe are not conducive to taking risks. Teachers who use traditional grading structures, inadvertently, model the process of judging students. Since risk is an essential ingredient for optimal language exploration, the ideal environment will encourage learners to have fun. Risk, when it is freely embraced, becomes a response to a built-in human urge to dare, to seek, to go beyond the known.

Risk-taking is a critical ingredient to the process of second language learning

Examples of Classroom Threat Include:

- **Anything that embarrasses students**
- **Unrealistic deadlines or expectations**
- **Uncomfortable physical arrangements**
- **Inappropriate rules or teaching practices**
- **Threat of harm or ultimatums**

What other forms of threat might your students be experiencing?

_____

_____

_____

_____

We are not talking here primarily of the more obvious overt, conscious verbal threats which teachers often make, but of the pervasive background of fear against which many of our instructional programs operate - fear of failure, fear of appearing stupid, fear of authority, fear of consequences of all kinds.

▼ 6 The Brain Thrives on High-Volume Input

There is a big difference between being taught with direct instruction methods and learning through acquisition. The approach outlined in this book favors acquisition. Biological evidence suggests that while we are astonishingly able to process massive levels of multi-sensory input, traditional instruction provides quite the opposite.

The human brain is highly sophisticated at prioritizing massive levels of information. It constantly sorts and resorts so that survival, learning and task optimization occur in priority order. Walk through a country fair, a discotheque, a shopping mall, a circus or sporting event and you'll experience many sensations. Unless threatened by something or someone, however, you probably won't experience intimidation, fear or overwhelm. Somehow your brain accepts all the new sensory input and sorts it in a way that makes for an enjoyable experience.

At Bell laboratories in the 1940's, a standard unit of information measurement was developed called BPS (bits per second). Based on Bell's standard, consider the miracle of your brain's everyday processing ability: your auditory track brings in up to 20,000 bits per second. Your tactile system can unify and respond to 30 million BPS. But the visual system is the real wonder. It can handle up to 100 million bits of information per second! A typical classroom learning environment supplies less than one percent of this capacity. The result is more than untapped potential, it is bored students who leave school thinking, is this all there is?

A significant design element in traditional education is teacher control. The enormous effort expended to control a population is perhaps useful in a prison. In an atmosphere, however, where learning and risk-taking is essential, high levels of control are a serious impediment. Some educators are concerned that high levels of input can hinder the learning environment. But experts say we do not have to worry about over-stimulation so long as the students select input rather than having it forced on them. High quality, high volume input is the raw material upon which the language learning brain thrives.

▼ 7 ▼ Our Primary Source of Learning is Nonconscious

Surprisingly, a great deal of what we learn and how we know it is not taught to us; it is simply "picked up." The process of acquisition allows for vast amounts of material to influence us through our senses. Since our brain is designed to pay attention to only one sense at a time, the other inputs exert a significant

There is a big difference between being taught with direct instruction methods & learning through acquisition

cumulative influence on our learning. We learned to speak our native language mostly by just hearing it. We learned how to do our job by trial and error with feedback from role models, people around us and countless subtle influences. Often we refer to this learning as common sense but it is, more specifically, a blizzard of implicit learning that forms the substance of our cognitive architecture.

The old days of "stand and deliver" are not only out of date, they are bad teaching. Today's teachers ought to be a catalyst for learning or a choreographer of curriculum, not a talking textbook. The best learning happens in the midst of immense stimulation, variety of experience, rich, multi-sensory real-life stimulation, music, role-play, art and movement. These influences tap into far deeper sources of nonconscious learning.

The old days of "stand and deliver" are not only out of date, they are bad teaching

8 ▼ Emotions are Critical to Learning

Today's research suggests that emotions are intertwined with cognition; and that emotions, in fact, drive attention, memory and meaning. While excessive emotions can impair rational thinking, the absence of emotion and feeling is equally damaging to reason and rationality. The old thinking of keeping the class's emotions in check or "having an even keel," is outdated. "Positive" emotions spur an excitement and love of learning while "negative" emotions block learning if ignored. Emotions, if orchestrated sensitively, can influence a lifelong love of learning or make us want to leave a class and never come back. In our culture, emotions haven't always been considered valuable; in fact, discounting emotions is a typical reaction of generations who were taught they "had to be tough to survive."

Reader's Reflection

What are some strategies you might use to engage positive emotions?

Multiple Memory Pathways Facilitate Recall

Our brain does not store memories, it recreates them, very approximately, every time we recall. We don't have "memory banks." Rather we have pathways for specific types of learning (see figure 1-B). Some pathways are more easily retrieved than others. For example, our brain is poorly designed for textbook, rote and semantic learning. Yet, it is this methodology that is the basis for much of the traditional second language teaching. More compatible with our brain is learning in contextual, episodic, event-oriented situations. The brain thrives on engaging implicit learning pathways including motor learning, location changes, music and rhythm.

Also important is the fact that for optimal learning to take place, the brain needs "down time" for internal processing. Though the formation of lasting memory takes time, the research indicates that extended focus time is detrimental. This principle suggests that we are better off facilitating shorter sessions and building passive times into the curriculum for the brain to process the rich input of a new language.

 ## All Learning is Mind-Body Linked

We learn as a complex, integrated organism - mind, soul, feelings, brain, arms and legs. Everything is one complex, adaptive system to the brain which creates and controls it all. Learning that is integrated into the body tends to be better integrated into life; it is easier to retrieve and longer lasting.

The brain's primary "messenger service" for information is not the commonly thought neuron-to-neuron synaptic connection. Evidence now suggests that over 98 percent of all the body's information is communicated through peptide molecules that float throughout the body. Each peptide molecule carries information with it and locks into receptor sites located in individual cell bodies. This binding process keeps the mind-body system working efficiently and in synchronization. The existence of this system strongly suggests the value of an integrated emotional, theatrical, physical, musical and environmental approach to teaching versus the solely cognitive, directed instructional approach used for so long.

In other words, sitting in a chair and getting lectured at is a poor method for learning a language. Acquisition is facilitated to a much greater degree by emphasizing the posture and motion that can actually be used to help communicate the speaker's message. All learning is dependent on the body's physiological state. Particular postures, positions and movements each store their own library of knowledge. Our eye movements trigger visual, auditory and kinesthetic thinking. Learning is affected by our heart rate, breathing and hormones. Our body is the nonconscious mind. It's time we treat the body as part of our learning brain.

We learn as a complex, integrated organism - mind, soul, feelings, brain, arms & legs

Figure 1-B

Multiple Memory Pathways

The mind/body connection is a critical pathway for memory formation and retrieval. 98 percent of all the body's information is communicated through peptide molecules that travel throughout the body. Each peptide molecule carries information with it and locks into receptor sites located in individual cell bodies.

Explicit

Includes both
- **short-term**
(5-20 seconds) &
- **working memory**
(seven +/- two)

Semantic
*words, symbols,
abstractions,
video, textbooks,
computers,
written stories*

Episodic
*locations,
events,
circumstances
"Where were
you when...?"*

Implicit

Procedural
*physical skills:
bicycle-riding,
body-learning,
manipulatives,
"hands-on"
learning*

Reflexive
*automated,
non-conscious
learning*

**Conditioned
Responses**
*"hot stove effect"
flash cards or
many repetitions*

Emotional
*intense
emotions...
from trauma
to pleasure*

▼11 *Our Social Brain Develops Better in Concert with Others*

Our brain has developed so that it is specialized rather than good at every-thing. Our primary communication skills are language-driven. Communication is a basic form of expression needed by the brain to actualize its potential and to generate feedback about the effectiveness of its programs. Speech - the ability to talk and understand - is probably the most important form of communication we have in this interactive and social culture. For this reason, it makes good sense for students to be encouraged to interact in class. Adults who aren't threatened naturally talk in class. Speaking can facilitate learning and understanding faster, especially in groups. Cooperative learning, role-play, dramatic expression, discussion, brainstorming and group projects all facilitate the learning process.

▼12 *The Brain Possesses a Language Instinct*

The human brain has biologically adapted to use language as a primary form of communication. It is a complex, specialized skill which humans develop spontaneously in every culture of the world without formal tutoring. Language is not passed down genetically, nor is it a cultural invention. It is not something that parents teach children, though most of them aid in the process. It is not something teachers teach children, though some may have had a minor role in developing language skills. Language learning is a gloriously natural instinct of all human beings.

The implications of this principal are profound. A preschooler's tacit knowl-edge of grammar is far more sophisticated than a phone book-sized grammar book or a robot with state of the art artificial intelligence. Children have the capacity to absorb, understand and store countless patterns of syntax, gram-mar and pronunciation before caregivers even know they can speak. They seem to carry recipes and formulas built-in from birth for the complex con-struction of language allowing them to create, from scratch, thousands of sentences by age three. Even preschoolers know, without any formal teaching, how to form sentences that make sense nearly every single time. And this hap-pens without a single grammar lesson.

The brain is good at learning grammar, but poor at being taught it. Why? the rules are far too complex for didactic instruction. For example, we all know a noun's a thing and a verb is something being done, right? Wrong. There are many exceptions to this common generality.

Language learning is a gloriously natural instinct of all human beings

> ### *These Are All Nouns:*
>
> - **The improvement of a city (an action can be a noun)**
> - **The shimmering was blinding (a quality can be a noun)**
> - **Mercifully, she kicked the bucket (no literal meaning)**
> - **The prime of forty-nine (an abstraction can be a noun)**
> - **A concert (an event can be a noun)**

Traditional directed methods of formal second language instruction, however well intended, are woefully out of touch with the brain's reality

These types of uses are so narrow, distinct, numerous and subtle that it would be impossible to teach them all (along with all the others in the language) by rote. Only through acquisition can a new learner make sense of them all. Yet that's what children learn to do every single day without being taught. What this discovery suggests, along with many others about the brain, is that traditional directed methods of formal second language instruction, however well intended, are woefully out of touch with the brain's reality.

Warning

Informed by the current state of research on the brain, we are beginning to have a biological basis for what many may have believed for years. But in spite of the tremendous amount of information we have discovered about the brain, more is unknown than known. Fundamental questions about how we learn remain unanswered by research in cognitive neuroscience. For example, we still don't really understand very much about the unconscious learning process; we don't know how much learning is stored in memory; and why individuals learn at such different paces. Hence, an acknowledgment of the limitations of current brain science is as healthy as our attention to it.

Summary

In conclusion, the purpose of this first chapter was to provide the reader with a framework for the brain-compatible language acquisition model which we call Joyful Fluency. The foundation of this model advocates a rich, multi-sensory, risk-free environment where the instructor minimizes error correction, increases non-verbals and doesn't force participation before readiness. Add coherent, social experiences with high input and a lot of feedback. Integrate music, drama, emotions and fun. Add a dash of real life, a cup of creativity and enjoy. While this may sound like a lighthearted way to introduce second language learning, there's more to it. In chapter two, we will review the related models of learning that have influenced the Joyful Fluency Model. ***Models are great learning tools aren't they?***

Introspection

What are my own feelings about the topics presented in this chapter? Why do I believe the way I do?

_____

_____

_____

_____

_____

Insights

What are some things I'm discovering now? What's the big picture?

_____

_____

_____

_____

_____

Practical Suggestions

What are the resulting actions that follow from my beliefs? In what ways might I improve?

_____

_____

_____

_____

_____

Chapter 2
Influential Models of Language Acquisition: Key Contributors

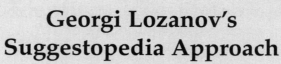

Georgi Lozanov's Suggestopedia Approach
Examined the role of:

Active/Passive Learning
Paraconscious Influences
Music
Suggestion

Barriers/Beliefs
Emotions
Healing Properties
Orchestration

Language Acquisition Theories

Stephen Krashen's Language Model

- *Instinctual*
- *Natural progression*
- *Low anxiety*
- *Importance of attitude*
- *Speaking follows listening & comprehension*

Tracy Terrell's Natural Approach

- *Balance between conscious & unconscious*
- *Communication before form*
- *Speech production follows Natural Stages:*
    - *Comprehension*
    - *Early speech*
    - *Speech emergence*

James Asher's Total Physical Response Approach (TPR)

- *Parallels first language acquisition*
- *Memory retrieval through physical body*
- *Language imprinted through movements*
- *Comprehension precedes speech production*
- *Never force speaking*

Influential Models of Language Acquisition

While it is important to understand the underpinnings of brain research and the framework for language learning, we must also know how to apply this information to develop practical language acquisition courses. This chapter examines some of the pioneers of language learning who have translated much of what we know today into practical strategies for the classroom.

The primary contributor to the Joyful Fluency Model is Bulgarian physician, psychiatrist and educational researcher, Georgi Lozanov. Lozanov's significant contributions include:

Key Principles of Lozanov's Suggestopedia Approach:

- **The examination of paraconscious influences**
- **The role of emotions in learning**
- **The use of music in learning**
- **Learning as transformational healing**
- **The use of suggestion**
- **The importance of active and passive learning**
- **Understanding learner barriers and beliefs**

In their book *SuperLearning* (1975), authors Sheila Ostrander and Lynn Schroeder documented Lozanov's second language learning successes which astonished the Western World. Some studies demonstrated that Lozanov's students achieved conversational fluency three to five times faster than those who were taught with traditional methods.

Certain music not only sets the mood for learning, but it also creates a dramatic background for hearing it, and a soothing state for embedding it

In addition, the powerful work of three other major contributors in language learning have strongly influenced the Joyful Fluency Model. They include: James Asher who explored the use of Total Physical Response (TPR); Tracy Terrell who contributed valuable insights on the sequence of language acquisition with his "Natural Approach"; and Stephen Krashen whose essential contribution was discovering the importance of rich real-world input. Each of these language learning pioneers contributed significantly to the synergistic mix that helps students learn languages quickly and joyfully. The purpose of this chapter is to acquaint you with influential methods that have contributed the Joyful Fluency Model; and to examine their practical applications in the language learning classroom.

Georgi Lozanov's Suggestopedia Approach

Georgi Lozanov has spent more than 30 years investigating and applying the phenomenon of accelerated learning worldwide. Once he understood the immense untapped potential of the human mind, Lozanov with his teaching partner, the late Evelyna Gateva, developed a program to utilize our mental reserves. This program has been called by various names including the Suggestopedia Approach, the Lozanov Method, the S.A.L.T. Method (Suggestive-Accelerative Learning and Teaching), and the A.C.T. Approach (Acquisition through Creative Teaching). For further study of Lozanov's work, please see the Bibliography. However, for our purposes now, let's review a few of his most relevant ideas with regard to the Joyful Fluency Model.

Lozanov believes that the brain, consciously and paraconsciously, receives, orders, codes, retrieves and utilizes outside stimuli in certain ways. He maintains that interpersonal communication and mental activity are always conscious and paraconscious at the same time. Paraconscious is that which is outside of our conscious attention, like peripherals, background music and subconscious associations. Because every stimulus is complex, it is interpreted, associated, coded, symbolized and generalized in a way that we can understand it. In short, everything reminds us of something else, even if not on the conscious level. This hints at the extraordinary potency and value of nonverbals, the physical environment, materials, and use of voice and music. In fact, these premises formed the basis for Lozanov's primary hypothesis regarding the crucial role of suggestion.

More than any of his colleagues, it seems that Lozanov understood the role of emotions early on. His work has always encouraged and even orchestrated the use of productive emotions. This fits well with current brain research which tells us that emotions drive attention, meaning and memory. Lozanov knew this and adeptly applied this principle through music, novelty, acting, celebration, suspense and role-play.

In fact, Lozanov pioneered the concept of music as an enhancer in second language learning. He describes it as a "binder" of knowledge; premising that it helps connect new words to their meaning more intensely than if the words were simply spoken without music. Certain music not only sets the mood for learning, but it also creates a dramatic background for hearing it, and a soothing state for embedding it. Lozanov advocates both Classical and Romantic music; and he is fairly specific about the particular types and timing for its usage. Many others, however, have found a wider range of music to also be effective.

Lozanov repeatedly speaks of liberating our extraordinary innate potential. He believes that an optimal learning environment can be transformational; that it should release and elevate us to states of joy. Influenced by the delight and pleasure which accompany the gaining of authentic new insights and competencies, he believes optimal learning leads to greater self-esteem, inner calmness, steadiness, confidence and trust.

These premises support the keystone of Lozanov's work which is known, overall, as suggestopedia, or the role of suggestion in learning. Lozanov says that "Suggestion is a constant communicative factor which chiefly through paraconscious (or subconscious) mental activity can create conditions for tapping the functional reserve capacities of personality." Once we know how to tap into the paraconscious levels of our experience, he believes, we will have acquired the tools for utilizing our extraordinary mental reserves. According to Lozanov, everything suggests something to us, and influences us on one level or another. Double-blind studies have shown that what we think of others does influence them, even from a distance. The power of thought has been documented; it can, for example, heal, hurt, move objects, kill bacteria and change a person's body size.

Thought is one form of suggestion. What we wear, how we care for ourselves, where we stand, the quality of our instructional aids, our choice of music, the intonation of our voice and our facial expression all represent additional forms of suggestion. What we suggest to others is a reflection of our beliefs and emotions which shape us. By purposely orchestrating this vast array of influencers, one can enhance the outcome of a learning experience dramatically.

New knowledge and skills need "incubation" time to allow for stronger synaptic formation and deeper memory "imprint"

Reader's Reflection

What other forms of suggestion might you use in your teaching and how so?

Another important aspect of Lozanov's optimal learning environment is the artful use of active and passive experiences. He begins a session, for example, with a strong, active, attention-getting concert reading which embeds rich, complex input on a deep level. Later on in the lesson, he might employ passive readings and role-play activations to tap into a different learning "channel". This method of variation matches up well with current brain research which tells us that new knowledge and skills need "incubation" time to allow for stronger synaptic formation and deeper memory "imprint."

Certainly one of the most insightful aspects of Lozanov's optimal learning environment is the delineation of the barriers to learning. He believes that our capacities are held in check by socio-suggestive norms, i.e., our conditioning. These social and cultural norms reflect the subconscious attitudes and beliefs of the world around us which limit our conception of what is truly possible. According to Lozanov, the ingrained, limiting attitudes and beliefs which each of us possess, to some degree, result largely from our childhood conditioning.

The kinds of barriers to which Lozanov is referring all have one common denominator - they operate to protect the seemingly safe and trustworthy status quo. To overcome them successfully is not to confront these barriers with something fearfully foreign, but, as Lozanov writes, "through harmonization with them." The three barriers Lozanov refers to are: 1) the critical-logical barrier which offers "reasons why something cannot be done (usually false); 2) emotional-intuitive barriers which evoke constrained emotional responses (like fear) to novelty and exposure; and 3) ethical-moral barriers which restrict our learning to those following strongly-held principles (like learning is hard work). Lozanov contends that until we deal with these barriers, we'll always fall short of our learning potential.

Reader's Reflection

How does Lozanov's model match up with your own?

In Summary of Lozanov

Lozanov's work is well supported by current brain research. He was far ahead of his time in offering both a global theory of learning and a set of strategies for helping students realize their potential. He provides a framework for allowing the teacher to begin to tap into the powerful subconscious resources we all possess, both as teachers and learners. The results, he reports in Bulgarian applications for both adult foreign language programs and children's reading and primary level math curricula, are quite dramatic. These applications have sparked the desire of many educators throughout the world to attempt to duplicate or adapt his programs.

Unfortunately, due to a repressive political situation in Bulgaria, Lozanov remained inaccessible to the West from 1979 to 1989. As a result, like-minded pioneers or interpreters were forced to proceed on their own. Although Lozanov's inaccessibility was regrettable, it did provide a positive stimulus for others, the author included, to develop further creative variations. Lozanov is now, as of this writing, able to travel freely and is once again in active contact with Western educators.

The Joyful Fluency Model is heavily indebted to Lozanov. Although it is recognized that the Suggestopedia Approach needs to be wedded with the constraints and possibilities of today's global cultures, Lozanov's work presents both a holistic theory of learning and a proven set of strategies for helping students realize their potential. The Joyful Fluency Model which represents a synthesis of the research is also informed by the following contributions to the literature:

Stephen Krashen's Language Model

Of equally broad significance, Steven Krashen's work helped language pedagogy catch up to the frontier of learning research conducted by people like Lozanov. Though Lozanov's influence on American foreign language education was slow in coming for various reasons including its inaccessibility, Krashen built a valuable bridge between Lozanov and the American foreign language teaching profession. Krashen, a psycholinguist at the University of Southern California, has offered a set of hypotheses on the acquisition of second languages. His work has made a decisive contribution to the development of the Joyful Fluency approach.

In Krashen's hypothesis we can recognize a kinship with the neuroscientists who call for massive, rich and varied input, (not logically sequenced) for optimal brain functioning. This hypothesis is well supported by the current brain research on limitations of visual, auditory and tactile information. We can also see similarities in Krashen's model to Lozanov's approach which advocates presenting large quantities of material with attention paid to context (multimodal, suggestive), and with little regard for grammatical sequencing.

Great care must be exercised to ensure that the positive student attitudes being so carefully nurtured in the classroom are not undermined through needless mechanical and boring work at home

Krashen's research supports the hypothesis that languages are acquired naturally and peripherally, not taught. He believes in a natural order of acquisition. For example, "He goed to the store" will be spoken before "He goes to the store." He also asserts that spoken fluency is driven by nonconscious fluency, not forced taught language. Language is learned by comprehensible input, focusing on the message, not the form. "Give learners natural communication," he says, "and if they don't get future tense today, they'll get it later."

Languages are acquired naturally and peripherally, not taught

In addition, Krashen believes optimal learning occurs with low anxiety and in learners with high confidence. He maintains that attitude is more important for acquisition than aptitude. This follows his belief that we all have input filters to encourage low anxiety. Finally, Krashen is adamant that production (speaking) follows listening and comprehension after what may seem like long delays in the learning. Krashen's work has held up well to the scrutiny of educators over the decades.

Reader's Reflection

Do you agree with Lozanov's & Krashen's premises? Why or why not?

Tracy Terrell's Natural Approach

The Natural Approach first developed by Tracy Terrell was designed to teach basic communicative skills. The approach has taken on added theoretical depth through close collaboration with Stephen Krashen. The jointly authored book, The Natural Approach, by Krashen and Terrell is an excellent companion resource for anyone interested in learning more about and facilitating second language acquisition. The theoretical foundation of the Natural Approach is essentially covered by the hypotheses of Krashen presented earlier. In practice, however, Terrell takes a more moderate position than Krashen regarding the distinction between language "learning" and the unconscious acquisition process. Whereas Krashen seems to focus more exclusively on the unconscious acquisition process, Terrell attempts to provide a greater balance between conscious and unconscious strategies.

Key Principles of Terrell's Natural Approach:

- Focus of instruction is on communication rather than on its form
- Speech production comes slowly and is never forced
- Early speech has natural stages (yes or no response, one word answers, list of words, short phrases, complete sentences)
- Teacher creates situations in which students are motivated to communicate
- Input must be interesting and comprehensible
- Understanding is more important than speaking
- Vocabulary development is more important than structural accuracy
- Absence of error correction is good
- Low anxiety is good

Low anxiety is good!

Terrell understands the language acquisition process as a sequence of three natural stages which are comprehension, early speech and speech emergence. Each stage has its own limits and possibilities; and it's crucial that the language teacher respects this.

Stage 1: Comprehension

In the comprehension stage, the emphasis is on student acquisition of vocabulary through physical responses, props, needs and classroom context. Using James Asher's TPR Approach (Total Physical Response) described later in this chapter works well at this stage because it increases the "binding." By "binding", Terrell means making a sufficiently strong association between new words and their referent so that the meaning is clear, felt, and therefore, remembered. For example, the sounds a student hears when the instructor says: "Setzen Sie sich auf den Boden!" (Sit on the floor!) is likely to be more firmly "bound" and remembered when the students actually sit on the floor in response to the command, than if the instructor were simply to tell the students that the words mean "sit on the floor." Binding can be enhanced through other methods, too. Terrell asks students to: "guess at the meaning of utterances without knowing all of the words used and without knowing all of the grammatical structures of the sentences." To facilitate this linking process, Terrell advocates the use of extensive contextual aids like pictures, props and gestures; and modifying speech slower with emphasis, and writing out key words.

Stage 2: Early Speech

This second stage commences when "students begin accessing and producing words and grammatical forms which have previously been bound through communicative interaction with contextualized input." Terrell asserts that in The Natural Approach environment, most learners will move voluntarily into stage two within two to ten hours of instruction. Typically, in stage two, you'll hear yes/no answers, one-word answers, lists of words and two word strings and short phrases. To facilitate the transition from stage one to stage two, instructors may use some of the following questioning techniques:

- Yes/no questions (Is Jimmy wearing a sweater today?)
- Choice questions (Is this a pencil or an eraser?)
- Questions which can be answered with a single word
  (What does the woman have in her hand?)
- Where? When? Who? questions

Stage 3: Speech Emergence

Terrell asserts that "after sufficient comprehensible input and opportunities to produce the target language in a positive environment, speech production will normally improve in both quantity and quality." This stage is characterized by a developmental progression moving through the following forms of production:

- Three words and short phrases
- Longer phrases
- Complete sentences where appropriate
- Dialogue
- Extended discourse (discussion)
- Narration

Activities to help students move into this phase can be more cognitively demanding like reading, writing and the study of literature and culture. This phase can be kept interesting by making sure the activities are life like and interactive.

Terrell's Stage 3 Activities:

- **Games of all sorts**
- **Problem solving using charts, tables, graphs, maps (i.e., Looking at this train schedule, how can we be in Washington, D.C. for dinner and stop over in New York City for lunch with a friend the next day?)**
- **Group discussion**
- **Skits**

Can you think of other activities appropriate for this stage?

_____

_____

_____

_____

A significant pathway for memory retrieval is through the physical body

James Asher's Total Physical Response Approach

James J. Asher, the developer of the Total Physical Response Approach (TPR), postulates that the second language acquisition process parallels first language acquisition. Asher maintains that the acquisition of a person's first language is greatly facilitated by the commands and physical responses which accompany the early exposure to language. Current brain research validates the use of total physical response in several ways.

First, a significant pathway for memory retrieval is through the physical body. This is known as procedural memory. We often recall what something is or what we wanted to do by simply getting up and moving. Second, areas in the brain that activate movement (cerebellum, frontal lobes, basal ganglia, motor cortex, etc.) are also well connected to the pleasure centers in the brain. Motion activates emotion; hence, moving can engage positive feelings and better retrieval. And finally, the peptide molecules which store information are distributed throughout the body. This means that almost any movement or motion can activate feelings and memories. This again, reinforces the learning and memory.

As with any
approach, the
"how" is
usually more
important
than the
"what"

The TPR Approach simulates, in fast motion, the stages an infant experiences in acquiring its first language. For example, before the infant utters anything more intelligible than "Mommy" or "Daddy," that child has experienced hundreds of hours in which language was imprinted through body movements. The infant may only be able to decode the language through the medium of body movements such as looking, laughing, pointing, reaching, touching, and eating. The understanding of the target language was achieved in thousands of intimate caretaking transactions in which adults gently directed the infant's behavior with sentences such as: Look at Daddy. Look at Grandma. Smile for Grandpa. Point to Auntie. Touch your nose. Stick out your tongue.

Notice that these transactions do not demand speech from children. The child is responding out of curiosity, need, or novelty; and because of the quality of the relationship with the parent/teacher. Usually, the child responds initially with a physical action exclusively; and as development progresses with simple one-word utterances such as "yes" or "no." Thus, the hallmark of TPR is the physical enactment of commands given by the teacher and/or other students.

One such TPR instructional strategy is to seat a few students on either side of the instructor and request, "When I say something in the target language, listen carefully and do what I do. For Example, if I say 'Tate!' and I stand up, you stand up. Just listen and act rapidly without trying to pronounce the words yourself." After using this technique, students are usually impressed that within a few minutes their comprehension has expanded rapidly. Within a few hours, students understand grammatical constructions that are nested in the imperative such as: "When Maria walks to Juan and hits him on the arm, Diana will run to the chalkboard and draw a funny picture of the instructor."

As with any approach, the "how" is usually more important than the "what." How sensitively an instructor uses TPR is crucial. Many if not most individuals are sensitive to power and authority and do not like being told what to do. The focus on the imperative form in TPR requires a skillful teacher to create a cooperative, playful atmosphere where students feel at ease and willing to fully participate.

James Asher, like Krashen and Terrell, holds to the basic tenet that comprehension precedes production; and all three recommend an essentially "silent" period of 10 to 15 hours during which a reservoir of comprehended input builds rapidly, providing the basis for the later natural emergence of speaking.

Key Principles of Asher's TPR Approach:

- **An understanding that language precedes speaking**
- **Comprehension is developed through body movements**
- **The individual will spontaneously begin to produce utterances when he/she is speaking**
- **Never force speaking**

TPR is a highly successful strategy, especially for the earliest stages of second language acquisition. While it exploits play and fantasy, student motivation and confidence build quickly as students succeed in demonstrating their comprehension through physical movements. Asher has also given us an excellent tool for engaging our students' physical energies so lamentably neglected in most educational settings. The physical aspect alone helps raise student interest and motivational levels. The playful nature of the commands and responses make this technique very brain-compatible. Finally, TPR is a relatively easy strategy to master and integrate into a wide variety of teaching approaches.

Summary

One can see much common ground between Krashen, Terrell and Asher. Further, there are many areas of agreement between the work of Lozanov and the others, too. Each has brought something valuable and unique to the table. Each has influenced innumerable foreign language teachers and students worldwide. One could venture to characterize all four positions (Lozanov's, Krashen's, Terrell's and Asher's) as a deep, emerging trend: an acknowledgment of the extraordinary capacities beyond consciousness, and a commitment to exploring the ways of tapping into these immense internal resources.

Whether these authors speak in terms of brain capacity, paraconscious resources or subconscious language acquisition processes, we can find a common recognition of both the potential and determining forces of nonconscious learning. In this and in the previous chapter, some of the guiding assumptions derived from contemporary brain research and the work of the contributors presented in this chapter are:

Guiding Assumptions of Combined Language Models:

- We have extraordinary learning capacities waiting to be tapped.
- An optimal learning environment is rich with multi-sensory, comprehensibly contextualized input and is not artificially or logically sequenced.
- Among our most valuable resources are those that are subconscious.
- Realizing our fullest potential involves tapping into and cooperating with our subconscious resources.
- Suggestion is an effective tool for mobilizing our subconscious resources.
- A relaxed, low-threat, low-stress environment is optimal for learning.

In education, traditionally a field that focused nearly exclusively on cultivating consciousness, we find pioneers who are pointing to the subconscious as the next educational frontier waiting to be explored. The great forerunners in depth psychology, such as Sigmund Freud, Carl Jung and Roberto Assagioli, have led the way in turning our heads to processes which elude conscious control. The author embracing this holistic perspective on learning, Proposes both a methodology which synthesizes our conscious and subconscious abilities and integrates what we currently know about *how* the brain learns best. Known as Joyful Fluency, this brain-compatible model presented in chapter three is revolutionizing language classrooms everywhere. ***Turn to chapter three and see what it's all about.***

Introspection
What are my own feelings about the topics presented in this chapter? Why do I believe the way I do?

_____

_____

_____

_____

Insights
What are some things I'm discovering now? What's the big picture?

_____

_____

_____

_____

_____

Practical Suggestions
What are the resulting actions that follow from my beliefs? In what ways might I improve?

_____

_____

_____

_____

_____

Chapter 3
The Joyful Fluency Model

We possess extraordinary unused potential

Physical response imprints memory

Brain thrives on massive real world input

Syntax & grammar will be acquired automatically

Relaxed, non-threatening, joyful environment

Occurring through informal, but sequenced steps

Teachers either limit or free learning

Comprehension precedes speech production

Facilitator:
- *Thorough competence*
- *Caring attitude*
- *Genuine enthusiasm*
- *Concern for student*
- *Rapport*

Environment:
- *Natural lighting*
- *Color • Visuals*
- *Comfortable furniture*
- *Living plants*
- *Fresh air • Stereo system*
- *Comfortable temperature*
- *No chalkboard*

Materials:
- *Integrated*
- *Concise & clear*
- *Easy to read*
- *Props & manipulatives*
- *Supplies well stocked*
- *Working equipment*
- *Multi media*
- *Music • Color*

Joyful Fluency Is Achieved Here!

Methodology:
- *Playful*
- *Humorous*
- *Real-life*
- *Fantasy*
- *Revelation*
- *Visualization*
- *Metaphors*
- *Music*
- *Games*

Use of Suggestion:
- *It's everywhere*
- *Student greetings*
- *Colorful materials & visuals*
- *Cooperative learning*
- *Influence student bias & limited thinking*

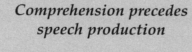

The Joyful Fluency Model

In chapter one, we took a brief look at current brain research as it applies to the acquisition of second languages. In chapter two, we explored prominent second language theorists and practitioners: Lozanov, Terrell, Asher and Krashen. From this framework, we will now examine the Joyful Fluency Model (JoF); and discover what commonalties exist and how to implement this approach to brain-compatible language acquisition. First, let's summarize:

Guiding Assumptions

- We all have extraordinary unused potential.
- The acquisition of languages occurs through informal, but definable and sequenced steps.
- The brain is designed to learn languages naturally - it's an instinct that does not require formal education.
- The optimal learning environment is relaxed, joyful, and non-threatening.
- The brain thrives on rich, massive real world input.
- Listening and understanding precede speech output.
- The brain can learn syntax and grammar automatically, most of it does not need to be "taught".
- We are all, in varying degrees, limited and conditioned by the beliefs we hold about ourselves, others, and the world.
- Involving physical response is an optimal way to begin learning a new language.
- The medium cannot be separated from the message: as teachers we model through every interaction what we expect from learners.
- When conditions are right, the student will spontaneously speak the new language - we should not force it.
- Students will learn the language better if the input is meaningful and the circumstances natural for response.
- Teachers either serve to reinforce self-limiting attitudes and beliefs, or they help students to transcend them.

Joyful Fluency Cornerstones

So, how are these assumptions turned into something meaningful - a curriculum that optimizes learning? The following five cornerstones are essentially what support the JoF Model:

JoF Cornerstones:

1. **Facilitator**
2. **Environment**
3. **Methodology**
4. **Use of Suggestion**
5. **Materials**

You will find that the above distinctions have crossovers. For example, although the "Use of Suggestion" is a category on its own, it also impacts the other categories and vice versa. Perhaps the single greatest influence on second language learning is the facilitator, so let's look in detail first at this cornerstone of the JoF Model.

Facilitator

With the influence of quantum physics, we may finally be emerging from a rigid form of scientific educational experimentation that emphasized rigorous experimental controls and excluded "subjective" factors (such as the teacher)

With the influence of quantum physics, we may finally be emerging from a rigid form of scientific educational experimentation that emphasized rigorous experimental controls and excluded "subjective" factors (such as the teacher). Previously, the paradigms used to measure the world were deemed only useful if they examined "objectively" what happened in a "scientific" experiment. Now investigators within the scientific community are beginning to acknowledge the essential, critically important, and desirable subjective factors (persons, teachers, researchers, etc.) in educational research. It seldom makes sense to speak of a method (the "what") without the teacher (the "how").

Even before Lozanov's work, Robert Rosenthal, documenting the "Pygmalion Effect" (see bibliography), provided us with the startling evidence of how we as teachers can largely and unconsciously determine success or failure in our students. We teachers have been invested with great authority - our voices, our eyes, our facial expression, our body language, our enthusiasm or boredom, our capacity to foster an engaging atmosphere (or its opposite), our encouraging attitude or our withering critical eye, our joy or our routine - the messages contained in such unconscious forces can literally create success or failure in our classroom.

To become aware of the tremendous power we individually possess and to take proper responsibility for it deeply challenges most of us, yet provides a wonderful opportunity for growth, as well. Recognizing our limitations and developing ourselves to be the best facilitators of learning we can is a major area of continuing development for the teacher using the JoF approach. It is the teacher who most profoundly affects the suggestive atmosphere of a class. Every teacher is an active and potent carrier of suggestion - whether s/he is conscious of that fact or not. The JoF teacher becomes highly sensitive to this fact, so that his/her impact may become consciously purposeful and constructive. In sum, the JoF teacher strives for the following qualities:

- Thorough competence in subject area
- Genuine teacher enthusiasm for subject matter
- An atmosphere filled with a caring attitude where fear is absent
- Genuine teacher interest in and concern for students
- Individualized appreciation for each student
- A natural sense of authority and self-esteem
- Mutual respect between teacher and student
- Easy, relaxed teacher-student rapport
- Playful atmosphere
- Humor
- Personal and professional style that is congruent with the purpose of the learning situation
- Use of positively suggestive language
- Positive, supportive group dynamics

The JoF approach involves a broad range of techniques not unique to any one particular model of education; however, an emphasis lies distinctly on the means rather than the end result - "how" versus "what." This shift in thinking poses a challenge for many teachers since most of us have been encouraged to think in terms of measuring results and assessing progress via predetermined goals and objectives. The JoF approach, instead, emphasizes that teachers move beyond technique and prescribed assessment to "a way of being" - a modeling of desirable qualities. This approach offers the teacher an opportunity to connect with both pedagogical and personal purpose which can be quite exciting and validating.

Environment

Current brain research demonstrates that the human brain thrives on an input-rich environment more than one that is just "logically" organized. Thus, the environment becomes an arena in which teachers can learn to facilitate additional significant learning. The JoF approach subscribes to an aesthetically pleasant, attractive, colorful, and comfortable environment that engages all of the senses.

Every teacher is an active and potent carrier of suggestion

The following suggestions go a long way in enhancing the Joyful Fluency classroom environment:

- The lighting, if possible, is natural or full-spectrum rather than fluorescent.
- The predominant color is a subtle green with yellow, orange, and blue used as highlight colors.
- The floor is carpeted which provides an important comfort factor, extends functional space, and serves to soften the acoustics.
- The walls have aesthetic, relaxing, and instructional visuals, such as pictures, maps, and posters which are changed regularly to complement the course content.
- Living plants and/or freshly cut flowers enhance the environment.
- Rather than conventional desks, comfortable chairs are provided which offer support for the arms and head.
- The room is well ventilated, properly heated and cooled, and has fresh not stale air.
- Easels, flip charts and/or white boards with color markers are used rather than a chalkboard.
- Classroom accents reflect the country of the language being learned (i.e., if you're teaching Italian put up travel posters of Italy, include or depict food samples like garlic and pasta, play Italian music and include a demonstration of culturally appropriate dress.)
- A stereo system in the classroom provides the ability to play various types of music.

Reader's Reflection

What are some other classroom enhancement ideas?

The above examples reflect a learning environment that pays as much attention to the psychology of the learner as it does to the students physiology. In the JoF model, the teacher constantly strives to suggest the possibility of a new and different learning experience both quantitatively, and qualitatively. Every effort is made to move students beyond past self-limiting attitudes toward joyful learning that liberates more of the student's potential.

Methodology

The human brain is not organized for linear, one-path thought but rather operates by functioning simultaneously along multiple pathways. With this discovery in mind, we can no longer support the notion of fixed or mandatory learning sequences. Each of us learns in a personal, highly individual, mainly random way. Any group instruction that has been tightly, logically planned, therefore will have been poorly planned for most of the group; and will inevitably inhibit, prevent, or distort learning.

Having said this, beware of throwing out the baby with the bath water; trashing lesson plans is not necessarily the answer. Rather, let this serve as a reminder that most of what your students learn will not be in your lesson plans. Ideally, a strategy known as "orchestrated immersion" will eventually replace the lock-step approach that so many of us know all too intimately. In the immersion classroom, everything speaks to the learner: the walls, the furniture, the activities, the other students and the subject matter. Optimal learning takes place when the learning environment closely reflects the experience of actually visiting the country(ies) where the target language is spoken. Such an environment would include authentic communication situations, complex problem-solving and travel simulations. Brain-compatible language acquisition methodology is always rich with meaning and includes a lot of student-to-student communication, thereby minimizing teacher-to-student lecturing.

The human brain is not organized for linear, one-path thought but rather operates by functioning simultaneously along multiple pathways

Orchestrated Immersion Ideas:

Lots of play!
Humor
Common real-life situations
Fantasy and imagination
Relaxation techniques
Visualization techniques
Metaphorical stories
Music
Games or role play

What might be other immersion ideas for your classroom?

_____

_____

The JoF Model emphasizes involving your whole class in scenarios that capture their attention. At early stages, it might be TPR. As soon as it's appropriate, involving the class in simulated real-life events like eating at a restaurant is productive. The more natural and complex the simulation, the better.

Use of Suggestion

We all enter a new learning environment with expectations, assumptions, and beliefs that limit our experience. For optimal learning to occur, more than "positive suggestion" is needed. Students are not blank slates awaiting input. They enter the classroom highly conditioned by past environmental influences. They have rooted beliefs about themselves as learners, about their teachers, and about the education process in general. Biases or feeling tones are attached to all past experiences. All current attempts at learning are heavily influenced by previous attempts which contain a vast array of stored biases. Rather than attempting to change undesirable behaviors directly, the JoF Model speaks to changing biases, therefore, influencing behaviors.

In other words, instead of forcing more accountability on students to learn, change the attitude. Persuade learners that learning a new language is easy, natural and valuable. It sounds simple, and it is. It takes a well-orchestrated campaign of constant positive suggestion to change the learner's attitudes. But once that's been done, the rate at which the learner can absorb new information is surprising, even breathtaking.

Lozanov, too, speaks repeatedly of the need to assist students in transcending their limitations; and he stresses the need for the de-suggestive/suggestive process which can help students replace limiting images and attitudes with liberating ones. Of all the practices advocated by the JoF approach none is more important than the use of positive suggestion to orchestrate an optimal learning environment. Suggestion is everywhere. This powerful tool has the unique ability of helping students transcend their limiting self-concepts, beliefs and fears. And, in the case of most students, these internal limiters prevent them from fully realizing their learning capacity. Just as self-limiting beliefs are percolated in the subconscious, so too is the power of positive suggestion. Research supports the conclusion that if we feel safe, confident, attractive, interested and playful within a learning environment, we will learn more rapidly and effectively. The following examples represent strategies for influencing students' with positive suggestion:

If we feel safe, confident, attractive, interested and playful within a learning environment, we will learn more rapidly and effectively

Examples of Positive Suggestion:

- **Greeting students at the door suggests that they are welcome and important**
- **Colorful wall posters suggest that the subject matter is interesting, intriguing and valuable**
- **Using teams, pairs and groups suggests to students that you value their interactions with each other; and their abilities to work cooperatively**

Materials

Lozanov was fond of saying "Suggestion is everything and everything is suggestion." Part of what he means by this is that there is no escape from the fact that everything influences everything else to one degree or another. The subject of materials provides a perfect example. The following either-or suggestions can be directly or indirectly influenced by the teacher's choice of materials:

- Learning is either easy or hard.
- The teacher either cares about you or doesn't.
- The subject is either simple or complex.
- The subject is either enjoyable or not.
- The students are either trusted or not.
- The learners are either capable or not.
- The audience is either worth the teacher's time or isn't.

Perhaps you're thinking, "That's going too far - students don't read all that into course materials." But think back to every course you've taken. Didn't you form impressions about the course from the materials? Didn't you say to yourself, "This is good" or "This is going to be hard!" Chances are, you did. The materials you use, therefore, ought to command just as much attention as the other precepts of the JoF Model. Not that materials are more important, but equally influential. With this awareness, why not suggest through your materials that learning is fun, the subject is interesting, the audience is capable, and the participants are trusted? The following examples reflect how you can integrate positive suggestions with your class materials:

Why not suggest through your materials that learning is fun, the subject is interesting, the audience is capable, and the participants are trusted?

39

Class Materials & Positive Suggestion:

- Use carefully selected texts and materials to ensure consistency
- Design easy-to-read, clear, concise handouts that include graphics or other visual design elements
- Use color when possible for greater impact
- Incorporate props and manipulatives that are fun, novel, and/or interesting
- Be certain classroom supplies are well-stocked and equipment is in good working order
- Use slides and overhead transparencies that can be seen from the back of the room, that are colorful and highly readable
- Incorporate music, multi-media presentations, and real-life simulations
- Review all materials before students receive them

Before distributing materials, ask yourself, "What might this suggest?" If you feel the materials suggest a positive learning experience, then proceed. If not, take the time to correct the deficiencies before lasting impressions are made. Once formed, first impressions are not easy to change.

Summary

This chapter presented the five key components to the Joyful Fluency Model: facilitator, environment, methodology, use of suggestion and materials. Chapter four will journey further into the role of environment. You may find it most comfortable to work with one component at a time; however, the components are interrelated. So, don't be surprised if you find other areas of your classroom management improving at the same time. As you begin to successfully implement these strategies, you'll discover many more fruitful approaches that incorporate the guidelines of the JoF Model. *Enjoy the process!*

Introspection
What are my own feelings about the topics presented in this chapter? Why do I believe the way I do?

_____

_____

_____

_____

_____

Insights
What are some things I'm discovering now? What's the big picture?

_____

_____

_____

_____

_____

Practical Suggestions
What are the resulting actions that follow from my beliefs? In what ways might I improve?

_____

_____

_____

_____

_____

Chapter 4
The Physical Learning Environment

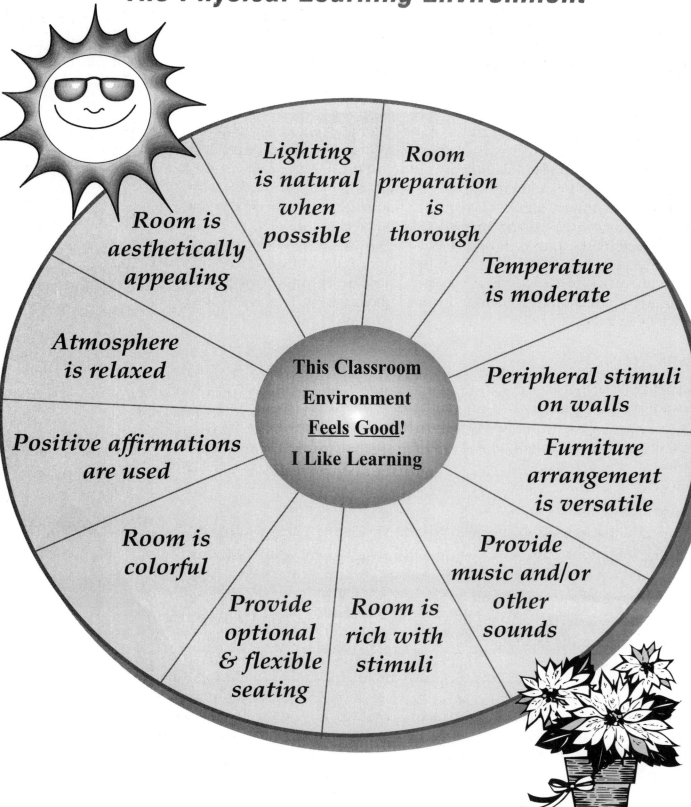

Lighting is natural when possible

Room preparation is thorough

Room is aesthetically appealing

Temperature is moderate

Atmosphere is relaxed

Peripheral stimuli on walls

This Classroom Environment Feels Good! I Like Learning

Positive affirmations are used

Furniture arrangement is versatile

Room is colorful

Provide music and/or other sounds

Provide optional & flexible seating

Room is rich with stimuli

The Physical Learning Environment

To the extent possible, the physical environment of a JoF classroom is aesthetically pleasant, attractive, colorful, comfortable, and engaging to the senses. Since the environment is a variable that can be easily manipulated, it makes good sense for teachers to take full advantage of it. The JoF approach advocates that the classroom be rich with stimuli, relaxed, and inviting. Students ought to be provided with an almost constant opportunity for sensory stimulation - things to hear, touch, see and smell - up to many times the amount of material conventionally introduced in traditional classes. Maximum attention ought to be given to creating a non-stressful, fully supportive and positively suggestive environment. In such a setting, students unconsciously begin to acquire a foundation for "understanding" before they even hear a word in the new language; in fact, even before the teacher first enters the room.

Room Preparation

As part of your pre-class preparation, ask yourself the following types of questions:

* Is the room neat and organized?
* Is trash thrown away?
* Are all chairs arranged the way they're needed?
* Are all the books and/or handouts counted and ready?
* Are all the materials spot checked?
* Is the room temperature comfortable?
* Is your course planning complete?
* Are greetings and student messages that need to be written complete?
* Are there happy, thought-provoking posters on your walls? Have you rotated the ones you've had up for a while to keep the atmosphere fresh?

A trash can by the exit may increase the odds of trash going in the right place and saves clean-up work. The rear of the class is the best place for a clock. Of course, there should be a clear policy about when the class is out - is it when the clock says so or the teacher says so? On the exterior of the door, a posted note should indicate to visitors or messengers what exactly they need to do before or upon entering.

Temperature Is Critical

Classroom temperature is often overlooked and is an essential element for establishing a comfortable learning environment. The first thing many people will notice when they enter the room is the temperature. Rooms kept between 68 and 72 degrees Fahrenheit seem to be the most comfortable for the majority of students. It is easy for a teacher to become so engrossed in what they are doing that they become insensitive to the temperature. For this reason it is suggested that teachers leave their class after each break to get a sense of the outside temperature. If at all possible, a teacher should find a way to provide good air circulation. Opening windows is the easiest approach if the weather and building design permit. Some teachers have found it helpful to attach a small piece of indicator cloth next to a window or air conditioner to inform them at a glance if the air is circulating.

For teachers who are interested and have access to them, ionizers and humidifiers have been found to enhance classroom comfort. About 20 percent of the population is affected adversely by atmospheric electrical charges in the air. Many experience great discomfort when the weather turns super dry and static electricity is high. A negative ion generator can be useful in these cases.

Use of Color

Classroom walls can be used to support useful peripherals and visuals. Simple enhancements can be made with color. The shades, tones and hues you use on the walls are important. Color consultants suggest that the predominant colors ought to be a subtle green with yellow, orange and blue used as highlight colors. Some teachers have found certain yellows to work well also. Colors create reactions consciously and subconsciously. A wood paneling or brick-face can also create a warm, home-like feeling in many cases.

Power of Peripheral Stimuli

Such things as graphic illustrations, posters, and charts which contain a mixture of informational and pictorial stimuli are cited as effective carriers of peripherally perceived material. Peripherals are subconsciously registered and later recalled when activated in the context of the larger whole. While the front of the room is really important to keep aesthetically pleasing, simple and uncluttered, the sides of the room are also of considerable importance. How often do you see your student's eyes wandering around the room? In most cases, very often! In one study, it was found that while the recall of lecture material went down, the recall of peripherals actually increased! Lozanov reports several experiments where he gave students a list of names to learn - requiring conscious focus of attention. He included peripheral information such as an instructional heading or color underlining which students were not

It was found that while the recall of lecture material went down, the recall of peripherals actually increased!

asked to learn or note. Subsequent testing showed that the material consciously focused on was forgotten at a rate predictable according to the so-called Ebbinghaus curve of forgetting. By contrast, the peripherally perceived information was recalled in a statistically significant rise in recollection.

For maximum absorption of your most important instructional visual stimuli, locate it on the sides of the room and up high. Do not draw attention to it - students will find it and learn quite well from it accidentally. Since peripheral messages are often more powerful than the standard front-of-the-room approach, be sure that all of your messages are positive and of the highest quality. When students are ready to learn grammar, peripheral posters will embed it. In class, present grammar learning passively; for example, in the form of attractive posters displaying structures and paradigms. A poster depicting a particular learning objective ought to be put up several days before any emphasis of the form is consciously made in class. Teaching at the semi-conscious level is especially important for subject matter such as grammatical correctness, a task which is traditionally conducted almost exclusively at the conscious memorization level.

Be very aware of the content of the messages you offer. Sometimes what you might think of as a benign communication may have ramifications not anticipated. For example, consider the experience of an excellent teacher who had a class of learning disabled students. She hung a poster with a nature scene and the message, "Things take time." Believing this would instill patience in her students, what actually came across was "you learn slowly, so don't expect too much, too soon." In another classroom a poster reads "School is something we sandwich between weekends." Here the message is that school "is something which gets in the way of things, and that weekends are what living is really for." Posters which inspire, challenge or enliven with joyous and supportive messages will add much to the class environment. A poster which says "You Can Do It" is much more useful than "Hang In There, Baby."

Reader's Reflection

What peripherals are you currently using? Are there others you might try?

Affirmations

Your room should provide students with a feeling of confidence and cheer. Posting affirmations is an excellent way to start. One strategy suggests putting 5 to 15 light colored posterboards up that offer simple easy-to-read reminders for your students. Write them in the first person so that the student reading them knows they directly apply. Posting such a sign above the door is especially potent. Change them often, and refer to them when appropriate. Affirmations work at the subconscious level and are useful regardless of whether your students are four or forty. The following represent some suggested affirmations:

Affirmations work at the subconscious level and are useful regardless of whether your students are four or forty

Affirmation Examples:

- **I am a bright and capable learner**
- **If you have learned something new today, give me five!**
- **Learning is fun, easy and creative**
- **I do new things simply, easily and playfully**
- **I am the change I want to see**
- **I am a unique and precious human being**
- **Every problem offers a gift**
- **I am a resourceful learner with many choices**

Lighting

Lighting is one of the most controversial areas in the discussion of classroom environment. It may be that each teacher has such different needs that it is difficult to obtain consensus. One point which most agree on, however, is that indirect lighting or natural daylight is best. Certainly some areas of the room have greater needs for light than others. Having sufficient light in the front of the room - on the facilitator, chalkboard or flip chart - is critical. Some have cited studies which indicate that full-spectrum lighting (natural or incandescent) is better than the fluorescent style.

Furniture Arrangement

Physical environment is strongly influenced by the arrangement of the furniture in the room. Unattached chairs and moveable desks are best for maximum comfort and flexibility. The chairs and desks that are used in most classrooms are an unfortunate compromise of price and quality. Most student chairs promote lethargy, back aches, poor breathing, neck pain and sore bottoms. Should you be in a position to influence the purchase of furniture, consider the relationship of physical health and posture on learning. The following offer some general guidelines for promoting good posture:

- Keep knees higher than hips when sitting in a chair.
- Rest arms and support shoulders when possible.
- Get up and stretch often.
- If desks are mandatory, sit close - three inches or less from your belly button.
- Adult chairs should sit 16 to 22 inches from the floor.
- Chairs should provide lumbar (lower back) support.

In a standard classroom, students with individual desks need approximately 10 to 15 square feet of space each; without desks, 5 to 8 square feet each is sufficient. If possible the classroom ought to be carpeted; however, if this is not possible, at least include a throw rug preferably in the front of the room. In general, also position yourself at the front of the room in a way that puts the least depth from front to back between you and your students. In a rectangular-shaped room, for example, it is best to stand at the center of the longest side. Moving from left to right "across the stage" or in the front of the classroom has more impact than moving front to back. Consciously set up the room in a way that best facilitates the kinds of interactions you will be encouraging. Room size is also an influential factor when it comes to environment. Most teachers do not have a choice about room size; however, there are ways to create the illusion of a larger or smaller room. The apparent size of a room, for example, can be reduced by using dividers or enlarged with mirrors.

Seating for Success

The key for seating success is variety and appropriateness. It's important to maintain a lively and varied set of stimuli and seating is an excellent way to do that. Where a student sits in the class affects his or her learning experiences, so the solution may be to allow for some flexibility. Some strong research by Rita Dunn and Kenneth Dunn (1992) suggests that many students will learn substantially better when given a choice of seating arrangement (floor or chair) and permission to stand or walk around if desired. Forced "frozen" seating can impair learning! Allowing students to choose a different seat each time they enter the room is one strategy for offering flexible seating. Remind the students that the room looks different from various angles and that they can gain additional insights and experiences by changing their vantage points. Switching seats may give students a fresh perspective; and may provide the impetus for leaving outdated limiting patterns behind. Arranging seating so that students can see and interact with each other easily is especially important.

Students will learn substantially better when given a choice of seating arrangement (floor or chair), and permission to stand or walk around if desired

Conversational distraction will lesson when the novelty of such an arrangement wears off conversational distractions will be reduced; and ultimately your students will benefit from the cooperative nature of the seating.

The Sounds of Music

The amount of stimulation that the human brain can receive and integrate is astonishing. What students hear in the classroom is just as important as what they see and feel. While your room may be visually attractive, 40 percent of your students learn best through sound. Hence, it is a good idea to include music and other auditory devices (i.e., storytelling, books-on-tape, nature sounds, etc.) in your lesson planning. Beyond affecting attitudes and evoking specific desirable mood changes, certain music has been shown to enhance learning and recall.

If possible, use a stereo sound-system with the two speakers positioned as high as possible in the room and secured to the walls or ceiling. Mask the speaker wire so that it is invisible and out of reach. The CD or tape cassette player you use need not be expensive, yet it should be dependable. It can be kept in a desk drawer or in a locked storage area when not in use. It is a good idea to have a variety of music types available. When deciding which type to play, observe the state of your learners. If they are lethargic and you want them upbeat, put on faster-paced music such as exciting movie themes. If they are hyperactive or restless, put on slower-paced music with 40 to 60 beats per minute. Some teachers play lively classical music at the start of class when students are arriving, slower music during moments of relaxation or test-taking and upbeat music during activities. Your choice of music at the start of class sets the stage and tone for the entire session; and ideally, increases your students' and your own receptivity for learning. Additional suggestions and strategies for the use of music in your classroom are offered in chapter six.

Summary

The JoF Model recognizes the vast importance of the physical learning environment. The physical environment, in turn, affects the psychological environment of learners. So in reality, the two are inseparable. Quite simply, when students feel good, learning is optimized. Such things as temperature, classroom organization, color, peripheral stimuli, subliminal suggestion, lighting, furniture arrangements and music all influence how we feel on a moment-by-moment basis; and these factors are usually well within our scope of influence. Not only are the students' mental states impacted by their surroundings, but ours as teachers are, as well. With this in mind, the importance of physical environment is obvious; and well worth paying attention to. In chapter five, we will examine how materials provide a crucial link to learning. *Teacher creativity is really an asset here!*

While your room may be visually attractive, 40 percent of your students learn best through sound

Introspection

What are my own feelings about the topics presented in this chapter? Why do I believe the way I do?

_____

_____

_____

_____

_____

Insights

What are some things I'm discovering now? What's the big picture?

_____

_____

_____

_____

_____

Practical Suggestions

What are the resulting actions that follow from my beliefs? In what ways might I improve?

_____

_____

_____

_____

Chapter 5
Materials:
A Crucial Link

Multi-Modal Reality Saturated Rich & Stimulating Materials

Props
Songs
Peripherals
Posters
Maps

Computer-aided learning
World Wide Web

Textbooks:
Primary & secondary
Custom or commercial

Magazines
Newspapers
Hand-outs

Videos
Music
Audiotapes
Transparencies

Guest speakers
Volunteers
Peer instruction

Materials: A Crucial Link

As discussed in chapter four, a JoF Model classroom will offer students a multi-modal, reality-saturated, rich and stimulating environment that enables the brain to do what it does naturally - to process large quantities of incoming stimuli. Exposing students to varied materials can increase motivation and stimulate new learning. Materials need not be defined only in the traditional sense: handouts, textbooks, and classroom equipment. Guest speakers, volunteers, or other teachers can also add a positive element to your enriched classroom. Inviting older students to assist you is another excellent way to expose students to many people; and having helpers in the classroom can help ensure that students get plenty of feedback.

Access to various computer hardware and software programs provides a very desirable option for students who learn best with immediate feedback and have an affinity for interactive electronic learning devices. Computers can serve as a "comfort blanket" for some students and as a rich source of content. The independent nature of computer assisted learning can be extremely beneficial for learners who prefer to move at a particular pace. Computers can be extensions of learning for the students or reassuring support for the facilitator. With the advent of the World Wide Web, classrooms can now link up with similar classrooms in other parts of the world. The implications this has for real-life learning are profound and obvious. This new territory for language learning has untold potential for making learning fun, reality-based, interactive, interesting, dialogue oriented, and student-centered.

Videos offer another form of enrichment material; and are often under-utilized. Exhibits, performances, demonstrations and field trips provide additional novelty and enrich materials. The more the stimuli, the better; however, it is also of critical importance that teachers believe in the effectiveness of the materials they choose to use. If editing, adapting and supplementing is necessary for you to feel confident that they are of the highest quality, this ought to be done. Your attitude will be communicated to the students whether you mean to or not. Using less than quality materials will likely frustrate any attempt you make to stimulate your students' highest potential.

Suggested Instructional Materials

The JoF Model is not a recipe; therefore, it does not prescribe particular materials. Your materials need to reflect your objectives and personality as the teacher. It is most important that you feel good about them and convey this enthusiasm to your students. The following guidelines ought to be viewed as suggestions only for generally compatible learning materials.

The Basic Language Acquisition Textbook

The task of creating genuinely interesting materials is crucial; as is, creating a context where learning can come to life

Two textbooks are generally appropriate for the language classroom. The primary text should be a lively drama that is filled with key vocabulary and situations for conversational re-enactment. Offering rich and varied input, this text ought to parallel the language banquet provided by the acquisition-oriented teacher. Its purpose is to aid "acquisition" more than to encourage "rote learning." Such a text can be purchased commercially, or you can create your own, or you can customize a commercial text for your needs. Whatever text you decide to use, make sure it includes a great deal of dialogue. And of course, it should progressively increase in difficulty. Most JoF teachers choose to substantially rewrite existing materials. The textbook occupies a central place in nearly every approach to language learning. Even if the focus is on oral communication activities, a written set of materials usually serves as the basis for elaboration and review. The more recent acquisition models, however, are less text-dependent although written and illustrated materials are still included as a valuable element in the instructional design.

The task of creating genuinely interesting materials is crucial; as is, creating a context where learning can come to life. All too often teachers criticize the "lousy" text or blame poor learning results on their lack of quality materials. Using materials that you feel comfortable with is your responsibility. A really good text that is full of stimuli might strike an initial chord of anxiety: "Is it really possible for me to learn all of this?", the student might think or "Is it realistic to think students can really grasp all this?", you might think to yourself. The JoF approach makes this leap however, without fuss because it proposes that maximal attention be directed toward creating a non-stressful, fully supportive and positively suggestive environment. In such an environment, learning will happen. Students need not worry about being judged, ridiculed, or put on the spot; nonproductive fear is, therefore, reduced, and the goal of acquisition can be well attended to.

During the first seven to ten hours of a class the JoF Model does not advocate using a formal textbook. Instead, it is suggested that words, phrases, and diagrams be written or sketched on an easel pad with colorful markers. Using this method, single sheets of illustrated conversational speech can be presented easily and effectively. Pictures provide contextual clues for comprehension. Gradually, single sheets of illustrated vocabulary and phrases can be given to students to supplement classroom activities.

Since suggestion plays such a central role in the JoF approach, your text or other materials offer a great opportunity to combine language content with embedded suggestions designed to optimize student learning. The principles and practices of using positively suggestive language in the classroom should be fully applied to the preparation of all written materials. Described in the next chapter in detail, the JoF approach suggests introducing the text to students in a way that optimizes receptivity. When this occurs, messages carried by the text will have much greater impact than material studied in a conventional conscious and analytical manner. Therefore, the importance of using positively suggestive language is multiplied.

Reader's Reflection

What are some of the positive suggestions embedded into your current materials?

Other Features Of a JoF-Compatible Text:

- The text should introduce 1,500 to 2,000 new words in the 90-hour Level 1 course.

- The text should include a series of approximately nine "acts" which comprise a coherent dramatic story with richly developed, authentic characters, situations and plot.

- The acts should be about 500 to 700 words long each with the first being the longest - introducing approximately 500 new words.

- The acts should be written in a dialogue format, in parallel columns, with the target language in the left column and the equivalent mother language in the right column.

*The text itself
serves as a
powerful
vehicle for
different levels
of suggestion*

- Grammatical constructs should not be presented in any formal fashion. Acts need to be written in simple, yet authentic language. Basic grammatical structures and paradigms should be included in the appendices. In this way, as students acquire a natural interest in grammatical forms and abstractions, they can obtain the information they seek.

- The text should be amply illustrated with images designed to suggest and reinforce the content being presented.

- On the left pages facing the dramatic dialogue, humorous explanatory words, phrases, drawings, cartoons, images or photos should appear that visually reinforce the suggestive purposes, enhance interest, and facilitate comprehension.

- The text should be "bound" in an attractive 3-ring binder. Various colors of paper can be used adding to its visual interest. The nature of the 3-ring binder makes it convenient to revise and supplement material as you see fit. Also, you can withhold pages to build suspense and interest in acts yet to come.

The text itself serves as a powerful vehicle for different levels of suggestion:

- The appearance (and format) of the text itself evokes suggestion. If you are using a custom-made text, students will pay a "materials fee" to cover the cost of making it rather than purchasing it at a bookstore. One of the benefits of this method is that the text can then be "presented" to the students all at once making additional unified suggestion possible. Also, questions can be dealt with right away at the time of initial exposure to the textbook.

- Within the text, direct suggestion should be used freely. The introductory and instructional statements can contain positive and encouraging suggestions to help evoke positive expectations. Such statements should be written in a confident, personable, helpful tone, inviting students to make rapid learning advances by tapping resources that they may not have used previously. Students are encouraged to enjoy the drama, participate play fully in it, and use it as a creative springboard for their own growing communicative style.

- Indirect suggestions are also embedded throughout the text. Characters in the drama encounter similar challenges, obstacles and frustrations (both literally and metaphorically) as students likely are. The way that the characters successfully handle situations - through their attitudes, their thoughts, and their statements - is projected throughout the material, often in the form of compelling images directed at the receptive subconscious.

An example of a character communicating indirect suggestion can be observed in a German textbook that features eleven year old prodigy who wins the hearts of the adults he interacts with, as he playfully and humorously models the behavior of a free spirit who loves to live and learn.

Commercial Texts

Many commercial language texts today are increasingly "communication" oriented and often provide activities which can be useful. Such texts, however, are still substantially different from a "suggestion-rich" text, which offers artful dramatic dialogues for presentations. Presently, the most brain-compatible language acquisition texts are part of commercial packages designed primarily for independent home use. As such they are, in my opinion, the best independent way to begin acquiring a new language.

A Supplementary Text

A supplementary text is important as a reference for grammar, structure, and syntax. While this text is of less importance than the primary textbook, it must still be user-friendly and quality-driven. While the primary text's emphasis is on acquisition, the purpose of the supplementary source is more aligned with the traditional side of language learning - to offer a clear explanation of the language rules. Also helpful as a means for writing practice, "learning" supplements do serve an important purpose in the JoF classroom. The danger, however, is in being lured by their authoritative structure back to assigning more traditional textbook learning activities; and expecting more from them than is appropriate for an acquisition-oriented classroom. Though I assign short sections of the supplementary text for grammar study and practice, I do not expect mastery through this rote learning approach.

Supplementary Readings

Readings that contain short passages can add richness and variety to your classroom materials. These might include magazines, journals and newspapers which are relevant to student interests. Such topics might include sports, fashion, romance and public interest articles. You may also include poetry or materials from other texts which may have only one or two items of value.

The way that the characters successfully handle situations - through their attitudes, their thoughts, and their statements - is projected throughout the material, often in the form of compelling images directed at the receptive subconscious

Songs

Songs have a wonderful power and magic to them. Consider some of the following options as additions to your other teaching strategies:

Song Uses:

- Sing songs in the target language that you know or have the music to
- Sing songs that your students know well in English, but ask them to re-write them and perform them in the target language
- Teach songs that have a dance step or theatrical element to them
- Teach songs that are found in musicals, foreign plays or popular films

Overhead Transparencies

Overhead transparencies can be useful on many occasions. They are most often used for the following purposes:

Transparency Uses:

- To set the stage for students entering the classroom
- To illustrate a point with humor or a cartoon
- To match up words and pictures
- To achieve a "big screen" effect or highlight important information
- To match the physical activity with the verbal command in utilizing the TPR Approach

Props

There's something whimsical, safe and engaging about props; and it's not just the teacher who ought to be using them. Keep a large prop box in the classroom for everyone to use. This is an excellent method for achieving a low-threat, fun and novel classroom. Here are some prop suggestions:

Prop Uses:

- **Hand puppets (particularly those with a mouth that moves as they seem to come much more alive)**
- **Costumes (need not be specific to the target language, i.e., uniforms worn by restaurant personnel are a good choice)**
- **Scarves, hats and glasses ("Groucho" glasses and nose work well)**
- **Wigs and canes (These items can be purchased inexpensively at your local thrift store)**
- **Clocks, maps, cards, empty cans, mugs, flags or keys**

Peripherals

As described in chapter four (The Physical Learning Environment), peripherals that you can hang on classroom walls make a powerful contribution to the materials aspect of your JoF classroom. Many teachers make a hobby of collecting colorful pictures on wide-ranging topics in the target language. If you are teaching German, for example, a poster or picture depicting a group of happy German people socializing at a beer garden might catch your eye. Or perhaps, pictures of German cars, castles, forests, rivers or cities interest you. Each of these images can help the learner integrate their feelings, vocabulary and culture with real-life language learning. Also, such things as graphic illustrations, charts and maps which provide a combination of informational and pictorial stimuli are effective information carriers perceived on the subconscious level.

There's something whimsical, safe and engaging about props; and it's not just the teacher who ought to be using them

Do you have other ideas for the use of props & peripherals in your classroom?

Summary

As with all components of the Joyful Fluency Model, we must be purposeful about what the materials might suggest to students. Every item suggests that either the language is hard or easy, the instructor either cares or doesn't, and so on. When you begin to assemble your materials, ask yourself, "What kind of associations might this evoke? Do I want these kinds of associations made in this course?" Remember, you have the power, at every turn, with every sentence, every transparency and every activity, to impact your learners. You can't *not* impact them. The only question is "*How* will you impact them?" What makes the Joyful Fluency Model so powerful is that very little is left to chance. In a well-orchestrated JoF environment, the strength of the teacher, the music, the planning, the joyful atmosphere, and of course, the materials create a synergy where students, virtually, *have* to succeed. Now in chapter six we will explore the various approaches for using language acquisition music in the classroom. ***Everyone loves music! It's the universal language!***

Introspection

What are my own feelings about the topics presented in this chapter? Why do I believe the way I do?

_____

_____

_____

_____

_____

Insights

What are some things I'm discovering now? What's the big picture?

_____

_____

_____

_____

_____

Practical Suggestions

What are the resulting actions that follow from my beliefs? In what ways might I improve?

_____

_____

_____

_____

Chapter 6
The Revealing Role of Music

Classroom Music Uses:

- *Opening class sessions*
- *Marking break times*
- *Enhancing guided fantasy & relaxation*

- *Community building*
- *Background stimulus*
- *Concert presentations*

Music Is A Potent Medium For Learning Joyfully

The Global Prelude

- *Overview*
- *Positive Suggestion*

The Passive Concert

- *To anchor new material*
- *Baroque music*
- *Relaxed state of mind*
- *Text not used*
- *Words **and** music*

The Active Concert

- *Music integrated with text*
- *Massive input*
- *Music from classic & romantic periods*

The Revealing Role of Music

In this age of "surround sound", nearly everyone turns on music to accompany moments of their day. For many of our students music has become such a habitual embellishment that one has to wonder whether a level of dependency or even addiction might be in operation. Though it is obviously outside the boundaries of this book to consider the merits of various musical forms; and at what point music listening becomes a crutch whether than an accompaniment, it is clear that music is a powerful carrier of culture in our world. Everything about music carries a message: the beat, the words, the associations, the performers, the era in which it was made, and the conditions under which is was recorded. For example, consider Elton John's song, "Candle in the Wind" written originally as a tribute to Marilyn Monroe. When Elton John rewrote this song for "Princess Di" after her death in 1997, it took on additional meaning. World-wide associations of loss, sadness, radiance, grief, tragedy, beauty, fate, senselessness, charities and car accidents, are now deeply embedded within this song.

The question I ask myself is: "How can I use this potent medium, to which my students are so sensitive, to pedagogical advantage?" My quest has led to years of personal experimentation with a wide variety of music for different purposes. Here are some of the ways I have found to use music to improve the acquisition of second languages.

Setting the Stage

Students come to class with varied inner moods and attitudes. Music can be a great aid in accomplishing the goals of: 1) distinctively opening the session or setting the stage for the class; 2) in establishing rapport; and 3) encouraging states that are learning receptive. Rather than students being greeted by a silent space where their possible negativity can easily continue, the infectious upbeat sound of the Canadian Brass Ensemble playing Baroque fanfares or of one of Mozart's bright Divertimentis greets them. I have actually watched the physiology of students change almost immediate when using this technique. The affect is quite dramatic: more color in the face, brighter eyes, more outward posture. The following selections are great for opening a class session.

Certain music enhances the relaxed or fantasy-like atmosphere that helps students open up to the inflow of new information

Opening Selections:

- **Thus Sprake Zarathrustra (2001)**
- **Blue Danube (Strauss) • Fantasia, Disney**
- **Suites for Orchestra (Bach)**
- **Toy Symphonies (Haydn) • Musical Joke (Mozart)**
- **Desert Vision and Natural States (Lanz and Speer)**
- **Movie Soundtracks: Chariots of Fire • Superman**
- **E.T. • Rocky • Lawrence of Arabia • Born Free**
- **Dr. Zhivago • Oh! What a Beautiful Morning - Oklahoma Soundtrack**

Music to Enhance Guided Fantasies and Relaxation

Certain music enhances the relaxed or fantasy-like atmosphere that helps students open up to the inflow of new information. After a few experiences students will begin to drop into deep, relaxed receptivity within a few minutes of focusing on the music. Here the music needs to be matched to the mood you want to evoke. It might be ethereal, moving, light, playful, powerful, swirling or moody.

Relaxation Selections:

- **Silk Road (Kitaro) • All recordings (Kobialka)**
- **SeaPeace (Georgia Kelly)**
- **All four of the "Seasons" recordings (George Winston)**
- **All recordings (Steven Halpern)**

Break and Transit Time

When it's time for a short break or time to leave at the end of the day, more upbeat popular music is usually well received. As always, you have some serious considerations in choosing the music. What do the words say? Are they in alignment with the other messages you're giving the students? What is the beat? Would you consider it slow, medium or fast? Does that pacing fit with the mood you want to set? Is the music in the target language? There's nothing wrong with using fun, more popular music, but it must be chosen with care and forethought.

Break Selections:

- **Hooked on Classics**
- **1812 Overture (Tchaikowsky)**
- **William Tell Overture (Rossini)**
- **Peanuts Theme (Giraldi or Benoit)**

Community-Building

A technique to build community is to introduce some songs without musical accompaniment. Using a spontaneous discovery type of approach, the class starts singing and moves towards a key which, as a group, they can manage. Such "creating it in the moment" learning with music has a fun, invitational quality that no polished recording can match. Though professional recordings provide a wonderful dimension of variety, scope and standard, do not forget to be creative in the process. Folksongs, popular songs, classical art songs, and folkdances can also add an element of creativity in your use of music. In-class folkdancing is a great technique for boosting energy and group bonding. Because my students are learning German, I use everything from German beer drinking songs, Marlene Dietrich and Lotta Lenya to Dietrich Fischer Dicskau and Nena with "99 Luftballons."

Music is a way to embed the massive input of vocabulary, syntax and grammar so that the learner's brain can absorb it all

Other Community-Building Selections:

- **Disney Soundtracks • Hap Palmer Songs**
- **Hokey Pokey • Million Bottles of Beer**
- **Camp Songs like, "She'll Be Comin' Around the Mountain"**

General Background Music

Though a few people may find background music distracting, the vast majority of students benefit from a consistent barely audible instrumental music selection in the background. I inadvertently discovered that playing certain low-volume classical music during much of the class had a very positive effect on students, a rather startling discovery for me who has always disliked elevator and retail store "Muzak." In fact, I had always found any background music distracting, possibly because as a trained musician, I tended to focus on listening to the music rather than on what was intended to be happening in the foreground. After forgetting to turn off the music I had played at a break, I discovered that it was noticed by students when the tape came to an end and shut off abruptly. Students suggested we continue playing the music. I, too, began noticing that the environment without the music felt suddenly "bare" and less relaxing.

Thus, I began to experiment with playing intentional background music at a barely audible level and noticing how it helped group attunement and rapport; and how it provided a cohesive element that was noticeably lacking when it was not there. I found that classical music was especially effective. I began to use it for my own tuning, pacing, rhythm, speaking level; and to bridge subtle but significant learning relationships. Music that has dramatic highs and lows is more difficult to manage as a backdrop due to its inconsistent nature. It is either inaudible or too obtrusive. For the purpose of background music only, therefore, you may want to use compositions that are steady and predictable. Compositions from the Baroque era offer some good choices. If you're going to use music from other eras, review them carefully first.

Personally, I have found some Mozart selections to be a good choice for background music. Over the years, I have typically conducted an exercise with my workshop participants where I play three to four minutes of Mozart's Divertimento for Strings, K.136 as purely a listening experience. Then I ask participants to share the qualities they would attribute to the music they just heard. Though I have conducted this exercise with at least twenty diverse groups of teachers from around the world, the list of qualities always looks strikingly similar. It typically includes the following qualities:

When I play Mozart at a just audible level, qualities such as spontaneity, vitality, order, and balance fill the acoustic environment of my classroom

Qualities Associated With Mozart Music:

Vitality	**Energy**
Positive	**Optimistic**
Dramatic	**Spontaneity**
Freedom	**Harmony**
Balance	**Humor**
Depth	**Joy**
Delight	**Playful**
Beautiful	**Imaginative**

This unified positive response led me to the natural question: "Would I like for my class to be characterized by these qualities?" Of course, the answer was affirmative. And of course, playing Mozart's Divertimento did not automatically transform my classroom into the above qualities; but on a subconscious level, students do begin to align and harmonize themselves with the environment's peripheral stimuli - music being one of the most potent. If it is rock music, we may begin to twitch our bodies and move our feet. If it is bright light, we may begin to squint. If it is Mozart's Divertimento, we may instinctively begin adjusting to the values it embodies. My working hypothesis is this: when I play Mozart at a just audible level, qualities such as spontaneity, vitality, order, and balance fill the acoustic environment of my classroom. With these qualities surrounding us, we subconsciously begin attuning ourselves to them; thus, supporting a learning-receptive environment.

I have no objective proof that my hypothesis is accurate, only my own subjective observations and those of other teachers who have experienced similar results. The feeling among teachers using background music as described above is nearly unanimous: they feel supported by it, the students like it and ask for more, and everyone seems more relaxed and more cooperative.

For the occasional student who complains (usually in the first week of class) that the music is a distraction, I promptly reduce the volume and suggest to him/her that shortly they will feel more comfortable with the low-level stimulus. I explain that the purpose of the music is to assist in creating a multi-modal, brain-compatible environment for enhanced learning, and that their feedback helps me to make an appropriate adjustment. It is important that the student feel heard and responded to. I always check in with the student days later to see if the music is still a distraction; and I have never had a student who continued over time to be bothered by it.

The most dramatic use of music in second language acquisition, occurs with a method known as "concert presentations"

Other Background Selections:

- **Four Seasons (Vivaldi)** • **Water Music (Handel)**
- **Brandenberg Concertos (Bach)**

"Concert Presentations" for Language Acquisition

The above techniques and music suggestions have enhanced the sensory variety and quality of my classes immensely; and they have provided a powerful stimulus to interact with the verbal component. The most dramatic use of music in second language acquisition, however, occurs with a method known as "concert presentations."

Remember how you learned the alphabet? For most of us, we learned the letters with "The Alphabet Song" to the melody of "Twinkle, Twinkle Little Star." The genius of using a song to learn 26 random, unrelated symbols in order is not complex; the melody serves as a kind of "binding" to help embed the words in your mind. This same concept can be used in language learning.

Lozanov theorized that music can be strongly wedded with words, thus significantly facilitating the encoding of material in the brain. After experimenting with a variety of techniques to relax students and suggestively present new material, he found that certain kinds of music provided both an ideal medium for creating a mentally relaxed state and for embedding the material into the brain. To take advantage of this synergistic effect, Lozanov conceived of the "concert session." Now many years later, the concert session is a proven method for introducing large amounts of new material. Usually, the presentation of the new material is presented in a global prelude-like form first; and then it is presented a second time with the information and music synthesized. This unique technique which is congruent with the growing understanding of the human brain and cognitive science discoveries is an important aspect of the JoF Model.

Reader's Reflection

What are some of your favorite uses for music in the classroom?

A concert reading purposefully uses music interplayed with planned content to create the effect, for example, of a movie, play or opera soundtrack. Well-delivered active concerts can open gateways to learning, reach the subconscious, create better understanding of subject matter, activate long-term memory and reduce overall learning time. The JoF approach advocates three stages or types of concert readings in language learning. A description of each follows:

Concert Presentation Stages

First Stage: The Global Prelude

Global preludes serve as excellent class openers. Whenever a new topic is introduced, use this preview technique at the onset to present the initial globalization - the big picture for learners. Set to intriguing, attention-getting music, the global prelude should be short, light and fun. It can also be presented as a chorus, parable, chant, or poem. The prelude builds confidence and anticipation. The optimal length is between three and seven minutes. The music and the teacher's voice are equal partners. The eyes' of the audience are open. A general sense of joy and fun should pervade the setting. Ordinarily, this "preview of coming attractions" has two purposes:

Purposes of the Global Prelude:

- **To swiftly provide an overview of the material and create a context for what is to follow**
- **To "suggest" indirectly to the student that what is coming is interesting, engaging, and comprehensible**

The global prelude is introduced by the teacher with an attitude of interest and anticipation. The teacher then mentions that they (the students) will be able to understand it with ease. He/she then "enacts" the basic content of the new unit, using appropriate props (objects, costume articles, pictures, posters) and pantomime. Brief broad-based questions can be fielded, but the atmosphere ought to remain joyful and light. The primary consideration at this point is to peak interest.

When the global prelude is effectively presented, the student experiences an intriguing performance where he/she is challenged in a non-threatening way to stretch her/his capacity to comprehend without expectation of comprehending. This process naturally increases the student's confidence and reinforces their emotional safety. At this point, the student is psychologically prepared to receive the large volume of content which will follow.

Peripheral aids in the room may also support the creation of a context for the learning progression. These may include posters with key phrases from the unit, colorfully written names and key words from the unit, or even grammatical paradigms which will be exemplified in the unit. The peripheral aids do not need to be brought to the conscious attention of the learners; this will happen on a subconscious level.

The presentation itself is a key factor for establishing success with the global prelude technique. In fact, the presentation is critical to every phase of the concert reading. If the presentation is done routinely or mechanically, unit after unit, the opposite of the desired intent may be achieved. It is of utmost importance that the prelude be delivered with genuine interest and delight, and with

When the global prelude is effectively presented, the student experiences an intriguing performance where he/she is challenged in a non-threatening way to stretch her/his capacity to comprehend without expectation of comprehending

a spirit of communicating something that your students will really enjoy learning. When an atmosphere of authentic communication is created, natural interest will further stimulate the learning process.

The next phase of the concert presentation is a more "formal" concert session which contains two musical presentations of the same material, each using different music and a different communication style, as outlined below:

Second Stage: The Active Concert

For this stage of the concert reading, music from the classical (1750 - 1825) and romantic (1825 - 1900) periods is used. Classic composers like Haydn, Mozart and Beethoven; and romantic composers like Brahms, Rachmaninoff and Tchaikovsky, provide classical compositions that are dramatic, emotionally engaging, ordered, harmoniously structured, and ending in a balanced resolution. Such music stimulates the brain and invites alertness while its harmony and order evoke ease and relaxation.

The active concert scenario occurs as follows: The target language, which the teacher is reading, is printed in the left column of the student's textbook, and the English equivalent is in the parallel right column. The new material is delivered by the facilitator in a specially intoned, dramatic fashion, guided by the music's tempo, dynamics, color, and phrasing. The teacher integrates him/herself as a special instrument with the other musical voices. The music is not intended as background. Rather, it equally integrated with the text, molded and woven together so that it is carried smoothly and as seamlessly as possible to the receptive learner. The optimal length of the active concert presentation is about 30 minutes. It is important that the teacher's voice not compete with the music. Rather think of it as "sound surfing." When the music pauses, you interject material. When the music becomes louder during the more active parts, you fade back.

The students' role is to listen to the concert presentation while viewing their texts. During the ample, frequent pauses in the reading, the student can readily glance at the right-hand column to check for the English equivalent, as needed. The active concert presentation is best presented with massive input - with much more than you think can be learned. This method is great for placing new material in context. It can complement the reading of plays, scripts or dialogue. Generally, teachers use the active concert reading technique once every five to ten hours of learning time. It is usually structured during the class to precede the passive concert phase described next.

Third: The Passive Concert

This stage of the concert reading serves as an "anchor" for the new material presented in the previous stage. The same information as was presented in the active concert stage is presented here again; however, it is set to Baroque

It is of utmost importance that the prelude be delivered with genuine interest and delight, and with a spirit of communicating something that your students will really enjoy learning

music (music composed from about 1600 to 1750). The slow, largo movements provided by the music of Bach, Handel, Vivaldi, Telemann, Corelli, for example, have a less personal, more rigorously structured quality than the later classical style. This music provides an optimal background of order and regularity which supports the more straight-forward presentation of material during this phase.

In the passive concert reading, the teacher reads the material naturally and idiomatically, guided not by the music but by the semantics and context of the text. At this stage you are the dominant player and the music is subordinate. The students do not follow the second concert reading with their texts. In fact, they are invited to close their eyes and experience the easy flow and mixture of words and music. They need only listen, remaining unconcerned about meaning or what they are supposed to be absorbing. The atmosphere should be relaxed. The passive concert session optimally lasts between 10 and 15 minutes; and it is always structured to end that particular day's class session.

At the conclusion of the second concert, I allow the adagio music to continue playing for several minutes. This provides a chance for the learning to subconsciously anchor or sink in; and facilitates a slow, gentle end to the class. At this point, further discussion is not entertained. I usually end the session immediately afterwards with only a "Das ist alles fur heute. Auf Wiedersehen." (That's all for today. Good Bye.)

Such music stimulates the brain and invites alertness while its harmony and order evoke ease and relaxation

Concert Presentation Guidelines

Content

Make sure that you know your content well and are comfortable with the meaning of it. Tell the students what you'll be covering; give them a short preview of the material verbally. Do this even when you are using handouts of the material.

Music

Make sure that you have listened to your music many times so that you know it well. I've found that if I listen to it in my car on the way to work several times, I can start to predict all of the highs and lows. Learn how long the introductory movement lasts? When does it go up and back down again in volume? How about the pacing and tempo? Do you know when changes take place?

Create the Environment

You may want to change the lighting a bit. Have the learners stand and stretch, and do some deep breathing. Give positive suggestions of expectancy. Allow students to sit comfortably.

The most

important

phase of the

language learn-

ing cycle - that

of encoding the

material in the

brain - occurs

during the

concert

presentations

Credibility

Stand with presence, with the authority of an orchestra conductor. Announce the name of the musical selection and the composer. This will prevent listeners from being distracted in trying to determine which composer and selection it is.

Volume

Keep your volume access close to insure you can control it. Make the volume loud enough to fill in the non-speaking parts and quiet enough so that you can talk during the "down" times.

Pause

Get the attention of the audience. Create anticipation. Wait until the introductory movement of the selection is over before you begin. Usually it's from 5 to 35 seconds into the piece.

Dramatic

Make large movements and enjoy making a show. Finish with a dramatic statement or final closing remark. Be willing to experiment! Doing concert readings is a great way to have fun, be creative and embed some powerful learning. Repetition is the secret to comfort. And with comfort, comes confidence and competency.

Treat the concert sessions with a certain degree of ritual, giving them a quality of heightened, suggestive expectancy. The most important phase of the language learning cycle, that of encoding the material in the brain, occurs during the concert presentations.

Summary

Music is a way to embed the massive input of vocabulary, syntax and grammar so that the learner's brain can absorb it all. The textbook, stories or scripts are used to provide the expansive new vocabulary. In our earlier discussion of the language acquisition models, we found that a large volume of input which is not artificially simplified or logically sequenced, is essential to a fully functioning, healthy brain. Many researchers recommend increasing the volume of real, multi-sensorial input by factors up to ten times what students presently receive. Music can help accomplish this objective. The material to be learned is offered in a high-input, global presentation manner rather than in more traditional linear, logical way. Adding music to the curriculum is an easy and joyful change to make. Chapter seven will explore other teacher controlled factors that impact the JoF classroom. ***Let the good times roll.***

Introspection
What are my own feelings about the topics presented in this chapter? Why do I believe the way I do?

_____

_____

_____

_____

_____

Insights
What are some things I'm discovering now? What's the big picture?

_____

_____

_____

_____

_____

Practical Suggestions
What are the resulting actions that follow from my beliefs? In what ways might I improve?

_____

_____

_____

_____

_____

Chapter 7
Joyful Facilitator Skills

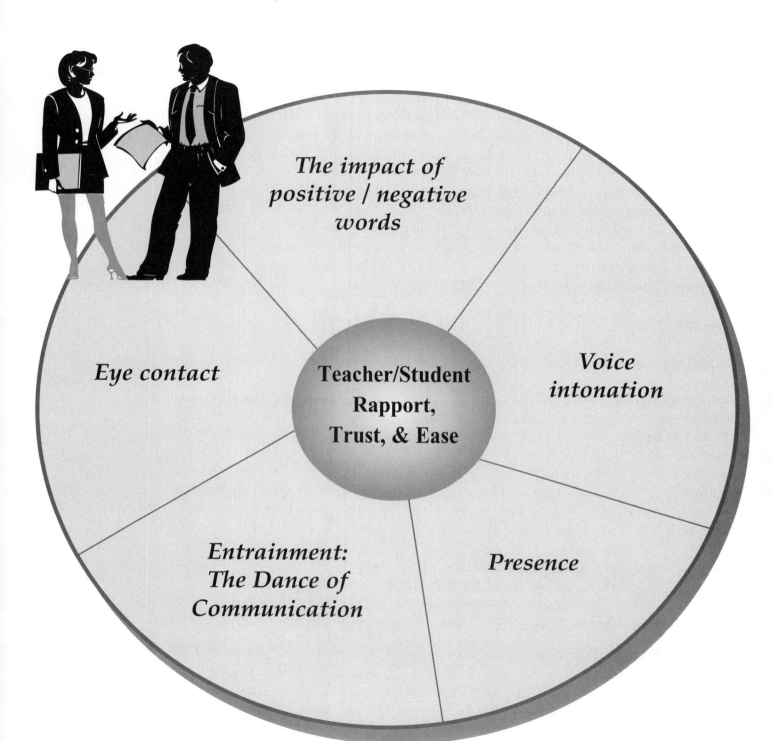

The impact of positive / negative words

Voice intonation

Teacher/Student Rapport, Trust, & Ease

Eye contact

Presence

Entrainment: The Dance of Communication

Joyful Facilitator Skills

As teachers today, our understanding of how to cultivate alignment, harmony, rapport, safety and authority in the classroom is much greater. The days of knuckle beating are behind us; creating a learning environment that is joyful, purposeful and respectful of learners is before us. We know how important it is for teachers to cultivate and maximally use a positive "presence" in class. Presence is the ability to gain students' respect so that your influence is effective. In the past, it was thought that presence was something teachers either had or didn't. However, it is clear that steps can be taken to improve a teachers quality of presence and build upon their current strengths. Successful teachers establish a way of being, a manner which suggests to the student a sense of rapport, trust, and ease.

One way to enhance the learning environment is to create a feeling of alignment in the classroom - a mutual understanding and acceptance of the class purpose. Partly this is done by using a "big picture" approach at the onset of the course. Students who are shown what they can expect to learn and how that will happen at the start will have greater trust in you as the facilitator of their learning process. If you don't know how their learning will happen, why should they believe it will? If you are sure of their learning, this will instill a sense of confidence in them that positively impacts their very ability to learn. Another method for encouraging this state of readiness is to take a few moments at the beginning of each class session for you and your students to get centered and fully present. Various meditative or centering exercises can help to achieve this, including teacher or student-led visualizations or a simple "check-in" from each person. I make it a point to take a few minutes alone before each class to center my own energies, letting go of distracting issues and thoughts, becoming as present as possible to the moment at hand.

Eye Contact

A simple but important awareness that has impacted my teaching is that of making conscious eye contact. As I began to pay attention to the "suggestive" impact of eye contact, I noticed how often in my haste or busy state I would meet the eyes of my students in a perfunctory way, if at all. When I began to see my students more authentically - in such a way as to say: "I have time for you", my students seemed to be more at ease with me. I am not speaking of a penetrating look, or one which demands or asks anything or tarries uncomfortably long, but a seeing which is relaxed and accepting - simply acknowledging the person as he or she is. Now, I take a few moments at the beginning of class to make eye contact with all of my students. Rapport has increased dramatically.

Positive Voice Intonation

Just as we have the ability to acknowledge, even embrace others, with our eyes, so can we "suggest" certain things with our voices. Our voice intonation often reveals much more than the words we speak. Voice tone is largely expressed and received subconsciously. As we become more conscious of our behavior we can begin to align this powerful vehicle of suggestive expression with our best intentions. In my own experience, it has had a very positive effect on my students.

When we consider the power of our voice, the centering techniques described above take on additional importance. If you are feeling stressed, anxious or frustrated, these emotions will be expressed unconsciously through your voice. Greeting students in a tone which expresses pleasure in seeing them and in being there has a very different effect than greeting students with a snort of negativity or a hollow hello. Of course, this is not to say that it is productive to feign such pleasure; students will surely detect the falseness, subconsciously, at least. Thus, the importance of centering and inner preparation is underscored here.

As my awareness regarding my own voice intonation has continued to grow, it has become a remarkably clear window into my inner state, attitudes and values. If I am truly aligned with my best intentions and purposes, my voice will express this alignment. Students, in turn, respond by being more trusting and willing to actively engage in the activities of learning.

Body Presence

Our physical presence in the classroom projects countless messages in a language our students understand fluently, albeit largely unconsciously. Learning to say with our bodies what we truly wish to communicate - aligning our physical expression with our true purpose - has a very positive effect on both ourselves and our students. In my early courses, I had every class videotaped. This provided me with the opportunity to see myself approximately as others see me; and it was a revelation.

At first I was very critical of all my idiosyncrasies and personal mannerisms. I noticed that my range of body movement was quite limited. I tended to stand or move in a small area. I gesticulated with my hands and forearms often punctuating points with a pointing index finger. However, as I continued to study the videotapes I became more compassionate with myself. It

Just as we have the ability to acknowledge, even embrace, others with our eyes, so can we "suggest" certain things with our voices

occurred to me that my growing consciousness was providing a wonderful opportunity for change; and I was learning to express myself more fully and purposefully.

To better understand the effects of my movement repertoire I watched the videotapes with the sound turned off. My physical language seemed rather impoverished; and, at times, dryly aggressive. I asked myself the questions, "How would I like to be?" and "What would be appropriate and purposeful in this teaching context?" In response, I began some visualization work and risk-taking in class. I tried out new movement behavior, such as allowing my body to align itself with the changing shades of enthusiasm in my voice tone. I began allowing more of my theatrical impulses to be expressed - opening my arm movements so that they gestured in an invitational manner instead of protectively, and so forth. One result was certain: I began to enjoy myself much more in the classroom. I know that if I am enjoying myself, the chances are that my students will enjoy themselves more. What now comes across on videotapes I have viewed of myself is a much less reserved, more naturally expressive, and more authentic teacher doing what he loves.

This personal example, hopefully, illuminates the importance of videotaping your teaching. Though, you may feel resistance in doing this, it is worth whatever discomfort you initially face. Then, find the courage and take the time to study the video, both with the sound on and off. Forgive yourself for any behaviors you dislike. Your objective is to learn from yourself. Make a list of what you would like to do differently. This intent ignites the process of change. Proceed by mentally rehearsing the specific changes you want to make happen. Recording the results in a journal or notebook will provide you with an opportunity for on-going internal dialogue. In doing such, you're reinforcing and imbedding your own learning.

Entrainment: The Dance of Communication

When we interact with others, we are doing so on two levels: the conscious and unconscious. Entrainment is the subtle physiological "echoing" we do usually on the unconscious level. To illustrate the concept of entrainment, consider that we all have times in our classes when everything seems to go just right. We feel understood and connected to the other person and what they are saying. We feel physically comfortable and alert, and mentally alive and at ease. Things just seem to click. And, then conversely, there are classes when we feel out of synch. We are just not on the same wavelength with our students. These two extremes of rapport (or lack of it) occur not just in our classrooms, of course, but in all areas of life and with everyone. So, what is going on in our communication that creates such different feelings and experiences?

Our physical presence in the classroom projects countless messages in a language our students understand fluently, albeit largely unconsciously

A good way to build rapport with others is to subtly mirror their body language

Partly, the subtle, largely subconscious physical changes we are experiencing as we communicate, echo or reveal our feelings as we interact with people. The concept of entrainment highlights the intimate physiological dance we do when we converse with another person. I became acquainted with the idea of entrainment through the physical act of "mirroring." As I began to notice how people in communication tend to mirror each other in crossing/uncrossing their legs and arms, tilting their bodies, and taking other matching postures, I began to consider how our body language suggests beyond our spoken words. As I worked with the concept, I learned that a good way to build rapport with others was to subtly mirror their body language. Eventually, I discovered the research on entrainment conducted by communication specialists William Condon (1982), Lawrence Wylie (1985) and Carolyn Fidelman. It was while watching an unrehearsed videotaped conversation between two native French speakers that I truly understood the importance of entrainment. The video which was transferred to a laser disk could be slowed down to punctuate the facial and body movements ten times or more without losing image sharpness.

From this perspective, much was revealed. When the speakers first greeted each other, their very different bodies, personalities and cultural styles were evident; however, almost immediately they began to adjust to each other. For example, one woman was smoking a cigarette, her conversation partner was not. The smoker lifted the cigarette to her lips for a puff, and within a split second, the other woman lifted her arm to scratch her neck in a gesture which strikingly mirrored the smoker, only without a cigarette. This "interactional synchrony" or entrainment did not stop at the level of large limb movements. Even more striking examples were observed in the speaker's unconscious facial micro-movements. Close-up shots of each speaker's face, simultaneously shown on split-screen video, made it possible to observe very subtle expression changes. I was amazed to see how the women even mirrored each other with their eye blinks, something that would go entirely unnoticed at the conscious level. Though physiologically, we do not need to blink more than every couple of minutes, in this example, the speakers usually answered each other's blinks within 1/30th of a second - totally out of the range of their conscious response time. Similarly, smiles and related mouth changes were also mirrored in split second fashion.

William Condon has noted that speakers' bodies move in precise synchrony with the articulation patterns of their own speech. The listener's body also modulates, within 50 milliseconds, to the incoming sound structure of the speaker's speech. As Lawrence Wylie elaborates, "It is an astounding fact that when two or more individuals are communicating their body movements are locked into synchrony with each other. Though silent, the listener moves some part or parts of his body precisely in rhythm with the voice and body movement of the speaker. There seems to be joint entrainment linking the two bodies during communication, even though this shared activity is out of our awareness - the more complete the interactional synchrony, the deeper and more thorough the bonding is between them" (1982).

With such a deeply involved dance going on, is it any wonder that we feel uniquely different in communication with one person over another? Truly, it is as if we are dancing with different people. With one partner we feel good, in-step and rhythmic; and with another we are completely out of synch. One of the striking implications of entrainment research is the realization that we communicate with our whole physiological being, not merely through talking. As Wylie further asserts, "Communication is a synchronized interpersonal dance." With some people we feel at ease and really get into the dance. With others we feel "jerked around" or stepped on.

Listening to our bodies can help us become aware of when we are in synch and when we are in resistance. When we are tuned in, we get the cue as to when something is "off" in our interactions; thus, offering us the chance to make a shift which can make the dance more comfortable. If we are coming from an egocentric place, or are holding ourselves back, manipulating, etc., we make it hard for another person to dance freely with us. However, if the dance is flowing well, it is probably a sign that we are in good rapport, entraining deeply, giving, taking, and exchanging messages at many subtle micro levels of synchrony. The lesson for me in all this is that I am setting the tone and creating the atmosphere for what happens in my class. The metaphor of the dance has been helpful. I often ask myself, "Is it probable that my students would want to join me in the dance I am leading now?" The answer almost always raises my consciousness and gives me more choices.

We communicate with our whole physiological being

Reader's Reflection

How do you think your students perceive the dance you are leading?

Approximately 20 percent of what we communicate to our students is transmitted through our words? The remaining 80 percent is transmitted via our posture, intonation, gestures, movement and facial expressions. Let's explore the implications of this for a moment.

The Transformational Power of Right Words

Words are prime currency in our trade as communicators. The value of that currency depends on how well it is invested. Our spoken communication with another person evokes in them internal representations associated with the words we use. When we speak the same language, we assume that the other person's representation is similar to our own, since without such similarity, communication would be nearly impossible. However, we may forget that the difference between individuals' personal representations is likely to be greater than we assume.

Our internal experience is represented in one or more of the following ways: visual (seeing), auditory (hearing), kinesthetic (feel), gustatory (taste), or olfactory (smell). Most of us have a preferred modality for representing our experience. Some of us are visually oriented and wish to see things "clearly." Others need to hear it, say it to themselves; and others convert experience into feelings and tactile representations. Very few represent experience primarily in the modalities of taste and smell, but these senses are also powerful triggers for calling up certain experiences.

When we communicate with other individuals, we can, as skillful communicators, match our language with theirs, in the interest of facilitating rapport and effective communication. When teaching in a group situation, however, individual matching is usually not practical; though, we can consciously learn to use balanced language which offers all students, regardless of their modality preference, opportunities to resonate with our language and establish rapport. An example of multi-modality communication might be:

"Good morning! As we begin to relax today, just listen to the regular tone of my voice and feel any tension begin to flow out of your body. Picture yourself in very calm surroundings and allow your eyes to move gently over the scene of your choice. Listen for the natural sounds which accompany this setting. Feel the agreeable temperature and textures around you and enjoy the feeling of ease and comfort while being here. "

Words are prime currency in our trade as communicators

The following list of predicates may serve as a reference for guiding the choice of language according to the particular purpose:

Visual Predicates:	Auditory Predicates:	Kinesthetic Predicates:
blackness	call	bind
bright	click	break
clear	clash	cold
colorful	crashing	cool
enlighten	discuss	dig
focus	harmony	feel
fuzzy	hear	firm
glimpse	hum	float
gray	listen	freeze
hazy	loud	handle
imagine	mellow	grip
inspect	noisy	grasp
ogle	quiet	hurt
paint	roar	nail
peek	scream	painful
perspective	shout	pounding
picture	silent	pressure
pretty	sing	push
preview	screeching	rough
see	squeal	scratch
seem	talk	solid
sketch	tinkling	squeeze
show	thunderous	stretch
vivid	told	unravel
watch	tune, tune-up	warm
witness	yell	wring

Our bodies, our posture, our predicates, even our tiniest movements are powerful carriers of suggestion

In short, our bodies, our posture, our predicates, even our tiniest movements are powerful carriers of suggestion. All play crucial parts in the magnificent communicative instrument which, as humans, we are. The good news is that we can get to know these aspects of our own communication better; and learn how to guide them into more purposeful alignment with who and how we want, as individuals and teachers, to be.

Our clothing represents another related aspect of communication beyond the words we speak. Our dress, grooming, and ornamentation speak volumes about us. Most of us are closely identified with the image we attempt to project through our external appearance. There is, of course, no "right" way to dress and groom as teachers, but clothing and appearance are important vehicles that can be used to serve (or detract from) our purpose as teachers. The following guidelines have been helpful to me:

Since I wish to be perceived by my students as a thoroughly competent and trustworthy authority; and since I wish to enjoy an easy, emotional and intellectual rapport with my students, I adjust my dress and appearance so that it is about one level more "dressed up" than the group of students I am with - not so much as to set me sharply apart - but to comfortably support my leadership role. Furthermore, I attempt to dress and groom myself in a way which will reflect the inner state I wish to project, without calling for others to notice me.

Summary

It is clear to me that the success of my lesson plan has much more to do with the rapport and atmosphere I am able to foster, than it does with the specific activities chosen. What may fall flat on one occasion may be splendidly successful on another; and the most important difference may be me. This means, I must take the time to prepare myself for my best teaching each and every class session. And, I must cultivate the skills and abilities to be present, in rapport and in synch with my students through all their ups and downs. Creating a joyful learning experience begins with the primary influence in the classroom - that's you (and me)! Now, let's look at how students form first impressions; and what we can do, as teachers, to influence positive ones. *Ready? Set? Go!*

Introspection

What are my own feelings about the topics presented
in this chapter? Why do I believe the way I do?

_____

_____

_____

_____

_____

Insights

What are some things I'm discovering now? What's
the big picture?

_____

_____

_____

_____

_____

Practical Suggestions

What are the resulting actions that follow from my
beliefs? In what ways might I improve?

_____

_____

_____

_____

_____

Chapter 8
Maximizing First Impressions

Assuming New Class Identity:
- *New name*
- *New role*
- *The "cocktail party"*
- *Fantasy*

Welcome:
- *Student expectations*
- *Overview of process*
- *Eliminate fear of failure*
- *Non-verbals*
- *Share enthusiasm*
- *Cultivate appropriate authority*

Impact of First Day Teacher/Student Contact

Body Learning (TPR):
- *Initial silent period*

The Room:
- *Attractive*
- *Comfortable*
- *Colorful*
- *Engaging*
- *Music*

Flexible Seating:
- *Impacts visual experience*
- *Affects group dynamics*
- *Keeps novelty high*

Peripherals:
- *Visual stimuli*
- *Unconscious learning*

Maximizing First Impressions

Though it is common knowledge that first impressions are extremely important, teachers (insured of captive audiences), often miss the opportunity to capitalize on our first contact with students. The first encounter we have with a class often sets the stage for what will follow. I have found that if I invest in the first day, the rewards come back ten-fold. Here's how I plant the seeds for learning success, and make that first day rich with positive suggestion:

Before the Course Begins

Even before the course begins, the success process is influenced by the student's expectations. Some of the factors which contribute to a student's expectations about a class are:

- His/her attitude about themselves as a learner
- His/her attitude toward teachers and school
- Opinions of his/her peers
- Course description in catalog, flyers, bulletin, etc.
- Teacher's reputation
- School's reputation

At first, we might think that we have no influence on a student's expectations before we meet. However, it is often possible to influence some of the above factors which contribute to the formation of a student's crucial inner set-up even before the course begins. Although, changing the school's reputation or even one's own may take a long period of time, we can usually have some degree of influence on other factors. It is relatively easy, for example, to positively influence learners by way of our written announcements about a course. A couple of examples follow:

- Create a lively announcement about the course and make it available to students and parents (bulletin boards, registration tables, enclosure in general school mailings, etc.) This can be done at any level.
- Suggest an interview and/or feature article in the school paper about the course, your approach, the innovative ideas, etc.

- Write a letter to each student who pre-enrolls in your course (or as soon as you have a class roster), welcoming them personally to the class. Express your own goals and describe your plan for the course. I have been told repeatedly by students how much they appreciated receiving a personal invitation to class, and that it very much influenced their positive expectations.

The First Day of Class

The first day is the most important of the entire class as first impressions are being made, attitudes and beliefs are being confirmed or modified, expectations raised or lowered

The first day is the most important of the entire class as first impressions are being made, attitudes and beliefs are being confirmed or modified, expectations raised or lowered. Such processes go on to some degree all the time, but it is in this first meeting that conditioned attitudes will be most changeable since reality has not yet completely confirmed them. Once set, the experiences to follow are likely to become variations on fixed attitudes, unconsciously locked away out of reach of most conscious attempts teachers use to motivate students.

Positive suggestions coming from a medical authority, for example, to a receptive patient can have a dramatic healing effect reaching far beyond whatever physiological problems might be involved. Teachers can have a parallel effect in helping students with their dis-ease in learning. At the outset, if a student suspends his/her self-limiting inner "set-up," s/he can begin to open to the possibility of a positive alternative to past negative experiences and perceptions. Suspended beliefs are the beginning of the type of liberating change envisioned in this approach. The following outlines some ways of maximizing the possibility for such liberating change:

The Room

The room can be a strikingly pleasant place to enter - attractively arranged, comfortable chairs in a crescent formation, colorful fabrics on floors and walls, interesting and visually engaging pictures and posters, ample but comfortable lighting, fresh flowers or plants, and music playing in the background. In short, as a student walks in for the first time, s/he is not greeted by "more of the same" but rather is pleasantly and invitingly alerted to refreshing, new possibilities.

Visual and Peripheral Stimuli

Peripherals promote acquisition learning because they give choice to a learner about when and how to receive and interpret the information. By definition, peripherals are the use of posted visual stimuli integrated into the instructional environment which the instructor avoids drawing conscious attention to. Dr. Lawrence Hall of Howard University has reported using these techniques to teach the Russian Cyrillic alphabet to students in just a few hours (1983). I am convinced by evidence that at a semi-conscious level the peripheral visual environment is absorbed in minute detail.

When we integrate linguistic content with visual images, thereby weaving stimuli together which stimulate both hemispheres of the brain for active decoding, we enhance and enrich the instructional environment. Thus, I create posters which blend language paradigms with decorative visual shapes (circles, triangles, arabesques), balanced in different colors. In my classroom, attractive, aesthetically pleasing ethnic landscapes and cultural scenes also surround language information posters. Such peripheral visual stimuli, however delightful and noticeable, once perceived and ordered at some level of the brain, begins to lose intensity and impact. So, I recommend that you rearrange and/or replace the pictures and posters and other visual objects about every three days as a way of keeping the room visually alive and intriguing.

We can allow the room to make its own impact before we appear. When my students arrive on the first day, there is hot water for coffee or tea relaxing music is playing comfortable chairs await them, and they can take a seat and absorb the unexpectedly pleasant atmosphere for five or ten minutes before I enter.

Student Seating

Another way to maintain a lively, varied set of stimuli is to change students' perspectives by altering expected seating patterns. If the room and class size permit, crescent seating patterns are far more preferable to conventional rows. When students are looking at each other, seeing faces and real expressions, they are much more likely to engage in real communication with each other. The conventional classroom arrangement focuses attention on the teacher and on the chalkboard. It is highly desirable to use seating patterns which encourage student-to-student as well as student-to-teacher interactions.

In addition, where a student sits affects his/her experience quite significantly. It also affects how we as teachers interact with him/her; and it can either contribute to fixed expectations or help transcend them. Students (like everyone else) are habitual about taking the same seat every day for the entire course. This is a lamentable and unnecessary fixation. Rather, utilizing "fluid seating" is an effective strategy for impacting students' visual experiences as well as group dynamics, general climate and novelty in the classroom. After the second hour, I ask students to choose a different seat each time they enter the room. I explain how the room will look different depending on the particular angle they are seeing from; and how the group dynamics will remain livelier and more interesting as we discover new neighbors and new faces across the room. Fluid seating is a powerful suggestive/de-suggestive strategy that can help students find fresh, unconditioned experience, leaving old limiting patterns behind.

It is highly desirable to use seating patterns which encourage student-to-student as well as student-to-teacher interactions

What do you do to prepare yourself and your students for the first day of class?

Many students come well-defended with strategies about how to survive the authority and demands of a teacher

First Contact

When I first enter a class and make initial contact with students, I am ready to give my full attention to the experience. I make it a point not to fuss with papers, folders, books, the chalkboard, and so forth. I am fully there with them and for them. I have taken time to inwardly center and prepare myself; and my body language, facial expressions and voice tone all communicate that. The message they receive is that I am glad to be there, I am prepared to be there, I am confident, and I am sensitive to their situation.

Non-Verbal Messages

I am generous with eye contact which invites communication. I thoroughly enjoy teaching and believe this attitude communicates itself in countless ways. I am clearly interested in sharing my enjoyment with the students. Such non-verbal messages are powerful and quite disarming for most students. Many students come well-defended with strategies about how to survive the authority and demands of a teacher. These unspoken messages encourage students to suspend old judgment patterns and join in the fun, at least as long as it seems safe. Keeping the environment safe is absolutely essential. Suspending old attitudes and beliefs is risky business until a safe alternative has been found - an alternative that can be trusted. Thus, in the beginning the students may respond with an often wary, provisional acceptance of what is going on. That is fine. Trust is made solid through time-tested experience.

Welcome

I welcome students both verbally and non-verbally. I express my pleasure at having the opportunity to engage with them in the unique learning adventure which lies ahead. I proceed to outline in broad strokes the novel and liberating assumptions upon which the course is based. I explain the exciting results they can expect to achieve - not on the condition that they work hard - but by virtue of their innate capacities to learn which can and most certainly will be tapped in this process. I assure them that this process has succeeded with many students just like themselves previously.

Eliminating Fear of Failure

After suggesting multiple images of success and enjoyment, I outline the simple requirements and grading policy for the course. Students are assured of a passing grade if they attend regularly. Thus, in a matter of minutes, one of the greatest barriers to learning, fear of failure, has been reduced. Students are then able to give themselves fully to the experiences offered without feeling a need to calculate possible grading consequences each step of the way.

Reader's Reflection

How do you share your love of your subject with your students?

Invitation to a New Language

The stage is now set to commence. I begin by sharing briefly with the class why I love the German language and why I love to teach it. I mention how much they have already been affected by the language and people of Germany (Einstein, Mozart, Freud, Marx, Hesse, Jung, as well as Hitler). I also emphasize how exciting and life-expanding it can be to open a window into another world through its language.

Immersion and Acquisition Begins

Next I invite students to relax into their chairs and listen to some "word-music" with me, just as an experience in sound. I recite a short poem by Rainer Maria Rilke and invite students to share the response it evokes in them. After several recitations I ask them to fantasize about what these words might be attempting to communicate. It is always remarkable how much students are able to glean from intonational patterns and cadences alone. I use this experience to point out how fluent they already are in the universals of language, and that they will be able to build on this grounding as they become fluent in German.

Evoking the Playful Child by Assuming a Fantasy Identity

After my students have experienced a positive first encounter listening and hearing German, I invite them to begin the adventure with me of acquiring this new language. The easiest and most enjoyable way to proceed, I explain, is to tap into their playful spirit. We learn best when we are mentally relaxed, and we are usually most relaxed when we're at play.

An easy way to play is to pretend that we are someone different than we really are. I then invite students to embark upon this group adventure by assuming a new name and life-role which can provide the basis for much fun and imaginative development. One or two large posters colorfully display German names. I read the names with considerable variety of intonational expression, asking students to imagine being christened Ingrid, Hans, Else, Udo, etc., and to "feel out" which name they would like to assume.

The Ceremony of Transition

Taking on a new identity provides plenty of opportunity for magical moments. I savor these moments with students, expressing my delight with their choice, repeating the name, allowing time for it to resonate and be fully acknowledged. The smile of delight on a student's face as they take a new name is always fun to see. Their assent to play as they call to another by a new name, becomes a powerful, positive rapport-building experience for students of all ages and backgrounds.

Why a New Identity is Important

If you want your students to act differently (more playful, open and risk-taking; and less suspicious and guarded), you will want to give them a "vehicle" in which to be different. In addition to choosing a new name; therefore, students are invited to select a new life-role. Lists of sample professions or roles are presented on colorful charts (i.e., dancer, lawyer, adventurer, pilot, ne'er do-well, monk, secret agent, millionaire, king, wise woman, etc.).

A very effective touch when students select their profession is to offer them a "prop" to accompany their choice: a crown for the king, a wad of paper money for the millionaire, a pair of dancing shoes for the dancer, a robe for the monk, etc. Rummage sales, costume stores, and thrift shops are often good sources for inexpensive props. Another approach is to ask the students themselves to bring a prop that symbolizes their new role.

The power of this technique lies in the student's acceptance of a new image and his/her consent to actively play. As mentioned earlier, this approach strives to promote disidentification from self-limiting beliefs and images.
Giving permission to play "as if" is probably not an adult student's normal experience in the language classroom, so the teacher must skillfully model a supportive, relaxed and playful atmosphere. Playing with a new identity can be a very liberating experience and students will respond in remarkable ways. Their ego-investment and self-consciousness will begin to diminish, and spontaneity and humor will soon take their place. The fruits of such an identity change become increasingly apparent as the students begin to embrace the fantasy and call on each other in their new roles. Indeed, every

time "Wolfgang" addresses "Udo" and the latter responds in kind, there is mutual assent to the play taking place. In an atmosphere of play we are naturally relaxed, alert and open - the key ingredients for rapid, holistic learning.

However, like nearly all techniques, the success of using a new identity for learning lies more in the how than in the what. Offered mechanically or routinely, a new identity might be accepted dutifully and/or awkwardly. Offered with imagination and delight, a new name and life-role can be a doorway that opens opportunities for freer self-expression, enhanced self-image and learning success. That such results happen in a JoF class is astounding (and freeing) to most students. As you implement this aspect of the JoF Model into your teaching, transformation will become an everyday experience in your classroom.

Reader's Reflection

What are some fantasy identities you might use in your class?

Anchoring the New Name

At this point, I lead students through their first of many singing experiences. I introduce a boisterous "identity song" with a preposterously simple "melody": Ich bin ich (I am I, you are you, he is he, etc.) The song involves much pointing and laughing, and as a result, students quickly become comfortable in playing with the "I am," "You are," forms they will be using in the following "cocktail party" exercise:

The "Cocktail Party"

The climax of this opportunity for personality transformation is a noisy cocktail party, replete with imaginary champagne, where students make the rounds introducing themselves in German, using a very brief cocktail party style:

Giving permission to play "as if" is probably not an adult student's normal experience in the language classroom, so the teacher must skillfully model a supportive, relaxed, and playful atmosphere

- **Guten Tag! Ich bin . . . (Hans)!**
  [Hello! I'm (Hans)!]
- **Guten Tag! Ich bin . . . (Ingrid)!**
  [Hello! I'm (Ingrid)!l
- **Freut mich, Ingrid!**
  [Pleased to meet you, Ingrid!]
- **Sehr interressant!**
  [Very interesting!]
- **Auf Wiedersehen!**
  [Good bye!]
- **Auf Wiedersehen!**
  [Good bye!]

These activities seem to violate one basic principle of the acquisition approach, that is, "comprehension before production." Encouraging students to venture speech production so early on in the course (before comprehension is realistic) is a trade-off for establishing group cohesiveness at the onset. Though not normally encouraged, this brief exchange in the target language is purposeful. The exercise is presented in a way that the emphasis is on the playful interaction rather than on accuracy. It occurs in a noisy room filled with other such conversations. No one is judging the quality of performance. There is much laughter, handshaking, even hugging. This exercise has multiple purposes: 1) it affirms the newly assumed roles; 2) it provides playful interaction that unites students; 3) it highlights verbal and non-verbal communication patterns; 4) it acts as a wonderful rapport-building device; and 5) it sets the stage for the many enjoyable group interactions to come.

Assuming a new identity is a simple language learning strategy - one which many language teachers have used in combination with various approaches. The potential of this simple transformation, however, is seldom realized or purposefully exploited by teachers. It remains too often a nice touch used only the first day of class; or the strategy remains underdeveloped and, therefore, never really accepted by the students themselves.

Reader's Reflection

Have you used identity role-plays in the past? Do you have ideas for expanding this approach?

Body Learning: An Initial Semi-Silent Period

The remaining time on the first day of class is spent using variations on the Total Physical Response (TPR) approach presented in chapter two. In the early stages of language introduction (especially while establishing positive group rapport), TPR activities work very well. Such activities include a series of gentle commands (actually "invitations" would be a better word) to students who follow along with physical responses. One TPR instructional strategy is to seat a few students on either side of the instructor and request, "When I say something in the target language, listen carefully and do what I do. For example, if I say 'Deka!' and I stand up, you stand up. Just listen and react without trying to pronounce the words yourself."

As a result, students are usually pleased that within a few minutes their comprehension can be expanded rapidly. How sensitively an instructor uses TPR is crucial. Many, if not most, individuals are sensitive to power and authority and do not like being told what to do. Hence, the focus on the imperative form in TPR requires a skillful teacher to create a cooperative, playful atmosphere, where students feel at ease and willing to respond to the teacher's "commands."

This approach is in full agreement with the advocates of an initial silent period. Remember though, this period is not designed as one where verbal responses are forbidden, nor should students feel rushed to speak. Rather, they should feel comfortable remaining silent, ingesting the rich offering of comprehensible input provided on these first days of class. Though, the students are largely silent, they are actively demonstrating their comprehension by moving, pointing, shaking their heads and laughing. Soon, they are responding with single words such as yes, no, here, there, you, me, he, she, it, etc. During this period, there should be no anxiety about correct pronunciation or sounding silly. The semi-silent period yields especially valuable results because a playful spirit is easy to maintain. This is a time when student confidence and group bonding builds very quickly.

Summary

The first day (or two) of class has/have been full. We've created a purposeful mindset with pre-course information, we've created a comfortable environment, we've introduced students to the overall plan for the course, and we've prepared them for learning success. Our first contact with students was planned and positive. We planted many seeds and dispelled many fears. We also got started with the acquisition process. A sample from the target language was read, new identities were chosen, and they were reinforced in a fun experiential exercise. The session was then concluded with further reinforcement through a Total Physical Response exercise. The day was a good one. Of course, you'll want to have a plan for the rest of the course, as well. An example of such a plan is outlined for you in the next chapter on Lesson Planning. **Get ready to put on your thinking cap.**

Introspection

What are my own feelings about the topics presented in this chapter? Why do I believe the way I do?

_____

_____

_____

_____

_____

Insights

What are some things I'm discovering now? What's the big picture?

_____

_____

_____

_____

_____

Practical Suggestions

What are the resulting actions that follow from my beliefs? In what ways might I improve?

_____

_____

_____

_____

_____

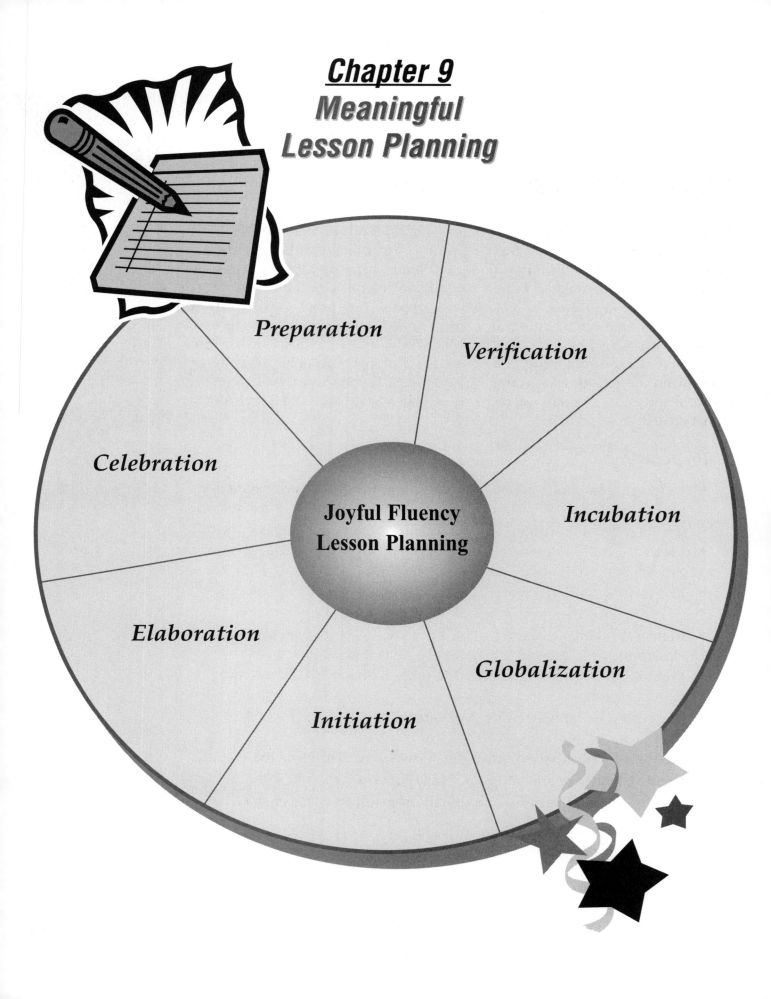

Chapter 9
Meaningful Lesson Planning

Preparation

Verification

Celebration

Joyful Fluency Lesson Planning

Incubation

Elaboration

Globalization

Initiation

Meaningful Lesson Planning

A single best way to format language learning does not necessarily exist. Many strategies will work as long as they are brain-compatible as outlined in the early chapters of this book. Having said that, some formats and strategies will encompass a wider range of brain-compatible principles than others; and will, therefore, encourage the brain to absorb, process and store experiences and information in a more meaningfully way. The following framework represents the seven learning phases of the JoF Model and offers suggestions for brain-compatible lesson planning. Each phase contains strategies that can be customized for various age groups, subject areas, circumstances and experience levels. Implement as many of them as is appropriate for your particular circumstances.

1. Preparation

- Help students create better conceptual maps by pre-exposing them to new topics hours, days and weeks in advance of the actual presentation.
- Create a strong immersion learning environment; make it interesting!
- Plan your class schedule, as much as possible, around optimum learning times based on brain-cycles and bio-rhythms.
- Learn about students' interests and backgrounds.
- Give students the opportunity to set their own goals.
- Make sure there are many colorful peripherals posted around your classroom.
- Provide brain "wake-ups" (cross-laterals, relaxation exercises and stretching time).
- Use strong metaphors and visualizations to encourage learning readiness.
- State strong positive expectations; allow learners to voice theirs, too.
- Create friendly relationships and easy rapport.
- Tune in to your learner's states; make adjustments as necessary.

2. Globalization

Globalization is one of the most critical parts of a lesson plan. It is what connects the learner to the learning. Similar to the "anticipatory set", the globalization step sparks curiosity and excitement.

Globalization is one of the most critical parts of a lesson plan

- Provide a context and "big picture" approach for learning the topic.
- Present the day's global overview, the themes, the interdisciplinary tie-ins, etc.
- Elicit what possible value and relevance the topic has to learners.
- Provide something real, physical or concrete in the learning process as the brain learns particularly well from initial concrete experiences.
- "Hook" learners with something novel that is also relevant and meets students' needs.

3. Initiation

The initiation step ought to include enough choice that all learners are engaged regardless of their preferred learning style. A far cry from "go home and read chapters four and five", this experiential phase provides rich subject matter for discussion. Though this stage may feel overwhelming to the learner at first, the massive stimuli gets sorted out in time, brilliantly - not unlike the real world of outside learning. Rest assured such a state of overwhelm will eventually be followed by anticipation, curiosity, and a determination to discover meaning for oneself.

- Immerse students in the topic - flood with input and stimuli.
- Eliminate singular, lock-step, sequential, one-bite-at-a-time information segments.
- Provide a virtual overload of ideas, details, themes and meanings: students ought to experience a sense of temporary overwhelm.
- Include a text reading in the active concert format, a guest speaker, a video and/or a performance.
- Provide interactive learning experiences (i.e., problem-solving exercises, computer-generated games, group projects, a field trip, interviews or hands-on learning).
- Employ all the senses as much as possible in the learning process: visual, auditory, kinesthetic, olfactory and gustatory.
- Base learning on discovery, student needs and themes; Allow students to discover something new that they're interested in; have them build, find, explore, or physically design something.
- Encourage students to attend a theater production in the target language, put on a skit or commercial, or create a newspaper.

4. Elaboration

The elaboration stage is when processing takes place; it requires genuine thinking. This is the time to make intellectual sense out of the learning.

- Tie things together thematically.
- Have learners write and pose questions to the class.
- Explore data bases on a particular subject.
- Use videotapes or other multi-media presentations.
- Facilitate group discussions and dyad exercises.
- Teach students to sort and analyze material through the creation of mindmaps.
- Use puppets, games, role-plays, competitions.
- Hold class discussions and forums for questions.
- Have students switch roles and play teacher.
- Conduct open-ended debriefings of the previous activity.

Reader's Reflection

Have we missed some important strategies? What might you add to our list?

5. Incubation

This critical "down time" should be used for unguided reflection. The brain is most effective at learning over time, not all at once. The brain needs time to subconsciously sort, process and connect ideas - to make meaning.

- Give students at least several hours or several days away from a topic recently presented.
- Include a physical activity during this period: stretching, walking, etc.
- Give students a day off, a recess, time for silence or music listening, journal writing or simply provide a change of subjects.

6. Verification

This assessment stage is for the learner as much as for the teacher. In this phase students get to demonstrate what they know. To be effective, the assessment needs to be personally relevant. Learning occurs best when a strong connection or metaphor makes the learning relevant. Giving students choices in the verification phase helps insure relevance.

Your lesson plans reflect who you are as a person

- Ask students to make a group presentation on the material they've learned or to prepare a lesson for the rest of the class.
- Utilize peer teaching and peer reviews.
- Ask students to design test questions.
- Conduct student interviews.
- Set up a mock situation like a customs inspection or traveling encounter.
- Have students keep a class journal in the target language.
- Have students create a working model, a mindmap, video, skit or newsletter.
- Set up role-plays; a game format is good.

7. Celebration

This phase instills the all-important love of learning. Never miss it!

- Engage emotions: use celebration rituals (i.e., toasts, songs, high-fives).
- Set up a time for class sharing: demonstrations, group acknowledgments, "breaking bread", parties.
- Listen to music.
- Bring streamers, horns, cookies and compliments to class.
- Encourage a class-designed celebration or outing.

Summary

Of course, it is not practical to expect to engage all of the above phases of learning during each and every class session. Nor is it necessary for your lesson plans to be completely pre-planned in a way that changes can't be made easily. Partly, the format you choose for each lesson will be determined by the time of year, current events, the class rhythm and tempo, student states of mind, and the needs of the particular group of students with which you are working. The above format is only a model for you to refer to, review and check your plans against as a whole. Your lesson plans reflect who you are as a person. Have fun with them. Let your creativity shine! Chapter ten will highlight the impact of purposeful suggestion which will certainly enhance your lesson planning strategies further! *Go for it!*

Introspection

What are my own feelings about the topics presented in this chapter? Why do I believe the way I do?

_____

_____

_____

_____

_____

Insights

What are some things I'm discovering now? What's the big picture?

_____

_____

_____

_____

_____

Practical Suggestions

What are the resulting actions that follow from my beliefs? In what ways might I improve?

_____

_____

_____

_____

_____

Chapter 10
The Power of Purposeful Suggestion

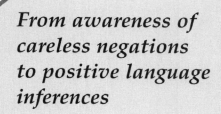

From awareness of careless negations to positive language inferences

- *Childlike Presence*
- *Curiosity*
- *Decreased resistance*
- *Tap into reserve capacities*

Doubleplaneness:
- *Multiple levels of consciousness*
- *Facial expressions*
- *Gestures*
- *Voice intonation*
- *Peripherals*

Purposeful Suggestion Can Stimulate Openness to Learning

- *Initial Impressions*
- *Appropriate authority*

Appropriate Authority:
- *Passion for topic*
- *No put downs*
- *Get to know students*
- *Subject competence*
- *Organized*
- *Quality materials*

Pseudopassivity:
- *Mentally relaxed*
- *Highly receptive*
- *Fantasy*
- *Alpha or theta brain states*

The Power of Purposeful Suggestion

Suggestion is the study and management of human influence. In one form or another, everything "suggests" something to us. We simply cannot *not* suggest. Our mother's face, a red jacket, a wedding ring, a poster of Tahiti, a bowl of chicken soup, the Harvard University emblem, a pair of Levi's, a new Mercedes and a set of chopsticks all evoke particular associations. We can't turn off our brain's natural tendency to make these associations; they are "on" every waking hour, and they can be a tremendous enemy or ally in the language learning process. In the Joyful Fluency approach we simply acknowledge these influences and positively manage them as much as possible. An increased awareness of the power of suggestion leads to more opportunities in which suggestion can be used purposefully to stimulate learning. The following influences and implications ought to be in the forefront of every teacher's awareness:

Authority

Your reputation as a teacher and human being, and the reputation of the learning institution itself represent powerful suggestive carriers. The teacher's perceived credibility, prestige, trustworthiness, confidence, and experience will naturally be summed up by students early on in the relationship. This initial impression will directly impact your level of authority in the classroom. Cultivating appropriate authority and a trustworthy presence is of major importance in the implementation of the Joyful Fluency approach.

Suggestions for Establishing Appropriate Authority

- Be passionate about your topic.
- Keep your word, tell the truth, be supportive, don't set double standards.
- Listen to your students, learn their names.
- Know the significant theories in your area of specialty or field of knowledge.
- Be prepared for class, start on time, personally check all electronic equipment for proper functioning.
- Be fully present and maintain a positive attitude; leave personal problems at home.
- Stay open to feedback and questions; never put a participant down.
- Acknowledge the work of others who have influenced you. Even if you are considered an expert in your field, remain humble.

When we evoke a childlike nature in our learners, resistance to new learning decreases and the desire for new experience increases

- Know your time limits and keep to them unless renegotiated with the audience.
- Use colorful, clean, innovative, professional quality materials that are up-to-date and well organized; be able to cite references.
- Share the success stories of others or personal stories that made you a better person.
- Develop your own show contingent upon the strengths of your unique personality.
- Stay current in your field; read trade journals, magazines and related books.
- Honor the diversity of your audience with appropriate references, words, introductions, materials and closings.

Childlike Presence

Evoking a childlike, playful state in students is an effective means of tapping into reserve capacities. As a child we had fewer fears and self-imposed limitations and a wondrous curiosity that allowed us to fail many times and still enjoy the process. When we evoke a childlike nature in our learners, resistance to new learning decreases and the desire for new experience increases. The potency of this influence is closely related to the degree of positive authority the teacher has in the class.

Suggestions for Evoking a Childlike Presence

- Incorporate new things into class activities at least once a week and better yet, daily. This keeps the childlike spirit of wonder alive in your classroom.
- Incorporate music that your audience probably heard as children (i.e., Disney or camp songs).
- Include games that your audience probably played as children (i.e., Musical Chairs, Simon Says, puppets, ball-toss). All can be adapted for any age.
- Include the use of paints, balloons, crayons and huge sheets of paper in classroom activities.
- Be expressive and react to novelty in a way that invites others to do the same.

Pseudopassivity

This is a highly receptive, mentally relaxed brain state in which students are easily able to experience and process information. You might recognize it as a fantasy state or as daydreaming. This "twilight zone" between being asleep and being awake is known as theta. A more active state that may be recognized as relaxed alertness, is known as alpha. Either of these are most likely to happen during the concert presentation technique described in chapter six on The Role of Music.

Suggestions for Encouraging Receptive Brain States

- Use guided relaxations with or without music in the first 15 minutes of class.
- Conduct active concert readings as detailed in chapter six.
- Use passive text reviews as detailed in chapter six.

Doubleplaneness

This is a term used to describe the multiple levels of consciousness in operation during any communication exchange. Though many factors operate below the threshold of normal consciousness, they are, nevertheless, exerting an often decisive suggestive impact. Such factors are numerous and include facial expressions, movement, gestures, voice intonation, pitch and rhythm, posture, etc.

Reader's Reflection

In what ways do you use the power of suggestion with your students?

Suggestions for Communicating What You Want To

- Match up your gestures with your words (i.e., the words "big" or "huge" call for expansive arm gestures).
- Use positive language; never use vulgarity, profanity, or make racist or sexist remarks.
- Dress professionally; be culturally appropriate; recognize the subconscious impact of what you wear.
- If students are distracted by such things as bad breath or body odor, they will not hear what you *want* to communicate.
- If students are distracted by expensive or gaudy apparel or jewelry, they will not *hear* your intended message.
- Learners will listen to you more consistently and acutely if you are always polite, empathetic, and use their names.
- Answer questions in a straight-forward manner; if you're not sure about something, explain to the learner that you will find out and get back to them.
- A firm handshake denotes confidence and certainty.

Peripheral Stimuli

A peripheral perception is a stimulus which has been perceived by the subconscious mind. Having reached the brain, this information emerges in the consciousness with some delay and is operative in tapping the learner's reserve capacities. This stored subconscious information underlies long-term memory.

Stored subconscious information underlies long-term memory

Lozanov reports several experiments where he gave students a list of names to learn requiring conscious focus of attention. He included peripheral information such as an instructional heading or highlights which students were not asked to learn or note. Subsequent testing showed that the material consciously focused on was forgotten at a rate predictable according to the Ebbinghaus curve of forgetting. By contrast, the peripheral information was recalled significantly better.

Having once entered the brain, there is a delay before the peripheral information floats up to consciousness. This peripheral unconscious information rests at the basis of long-term memory. This matches up well with the brain research which suggests that after learning, the brain uses "down time" to fix the neural connections better. This internal processing time works as long as there is no new competing stimuli to interrupt synaptic formation.

Suggestions for Using Peripherals

- Post colorful pictures on wide-ranging topics in the target language.
- Hang posters or pictures of happy people socializing, cars, landscapes, or other scenes that will likely be interesting to your learners.
- Put up charts depicting key grammar points.
- Incorporate fresh flowers, an aquarium or good scents in your classroom.

Avoid Careless Negations

Words function as mental triggers, and these triggers vary from person to person. When I say "elephant," an English speaker will automatically make an internal representation of an elephant. This representation is influenced by an individual's composite life experience with "elephants" and the associations accompanying them. Indeed, retrieval of "elephant" will occur even if we say: "Do not imagine an elephant." Go along with the following: "Do not imagine a pink panther!" As you probably discovered, it is not possible to make sense out of my words without visualizing some internal representation of them. Since our words trigger internal referents which may influence a student's performance and behavior in class, it is important for us as teachers to be aware of their evocative power. Thus, if my intention is to create a relaxed, non-stressful environment in the classroom, my words should be such that these feelings are evoked. Compare the following two class openings:

1. "Welcome! I am delighted to begin sharing with you a new approach to learning which is fun, relaxed, playful and effective. In this class we will naturally and easily tap into the extraordinary learning capacities we all have to learn; and we will discover how relaxed, positive and pleasant it can be."

2. "Hello class. Let's try and get started here. Oh, by the way, sorry I was late. I hope you will like this course. You don't need to be nervous or anxious about it. In fact, you can forget your tensions; and don't worry about trying hard. In this class we will attempt to go beyond our old limitations and leave behind our negative attitudes toward foreign language learning."

Which of the two statements above are more inviting? Contrast the following lists, derived from the two above statements, keeping in mind that each word is a catalyst for an internal process. Just what, specifically, that process will be for each student, we may not know, but we can meaningfully speculate about the general effect each statement tends to have:

Statement 1:	Statement 2:
Welcome!	Hello, let's try...
delighted	sorry I was late
sharing with you	hope ...like
new	need
fun	nervous
relaxed	anxious
naturally	forget
effective	tensions
tapping into	worry
extraordinary capacities	trying
we all have	we will go beyond
find	old
positive	limitations
relaxed	leave behind
pleasant	negative attitudes

Since our words trigger internal referents which may influence a student's performance and behavior in class, it is important for us as teachers to be aware of their evocative power

Although the intention may have been identical in both statements, the effect of each might be quite different. In the first remarks, the words trigger access to consistently positive areas of represented experience. In the second, the student will have to access non-positive representations repeatedly. Such images are likely to be incongruent with the quality of experience you wish to facilitate as a teacher.

Suggestions for Positive Language Substitutes

When I point out the differential impact that positive and negative messages have on learners, teachers usually comment that this is obvious. Yet, in my experience the majority of teachers still use words and phrases that evoke negativity and limitation. Here are some examples:

Unaware Teachers Use:	*Better to Use:*
Don't have enough time	We'll have time tomorrow
That's hard	This isn't quite as easy
Don't forget your homework	Remember your homework
You don't have to struggle	Relax and focus on this
Don't be late	Be on time
Don't do that	Please do this instead

An increased awareness of the power of suggestion leads to more opportunities in which suggestion can be used purposefully to stimulate learning

The subtitle of this section was not "Avoid *all* Negations." It was "Avoid *Careless* Negations." Although, there are times when negations are more suitable than the opposite, it is better yet to avoid comments that sting even when stated in the affirmative. For example, though a student would certainly rather be told they were "not a genius" than "you're stupid", perhaps, neither comment is necessary. Though, the first is a negation and the second, an affirmative, both are inappropriate. In another example, a student would rather hear that their work was "not yet perfect" than that it "contains noticeable flaws." In sum, awareness and attention to the evocative power of our words, and how they can support or undermine our pedagogical purposes, will enhance the power of our conveyed messages.

How To Tell When Positive Suggestion is Effective

Initially, you may wonder "Am I doing suggestion right? How do I know if it's working or not?" There's actually no mystery about it. When positive suggestion is being used and integrated with a well-orchestrated learning environment there will be noticeable results. Here's how to tell when it's happening:

- An individual's reserves of memory, intellectual activity and creativity are tapped into when they are learning in a positively suggestive environment. Students will feel "smarter" and will, therefore, act smarter.

- The teaching and learning experience will always feel pleasant. Instruction is always accompanied with an effect of relaxation or, at least, one without a feeling of fatigue. When the class is over, students will feel good, not wiped out.

- There's a favorable therapeutic effect; aggressive tendencies in pupils will soften. Feelings of joy or elation may emerge. An absence of tension should be obvious.

- Concentrated relaxation will be the norm.

- Acquisition increases. Students will discover that they are "picking" things up, quickly and naturally. A unity of the conscious and subconscious will occur. At the most unpredictable moments, students will find vocabulary and fluency springing forth out of their surprised mouths.

When positive suggestion is being used and integrated with a well-orchestrated learning environment there will be noticeable results

Summary

Excellent teachers, using whatever approach, will assuredly embody many of the positively suggestive qualities described in this chapter. They do so naturally and largely unconsciously. These qualities, which seem to be "natural" in some, can still be practiced and increased in potency. Once we understand how to align them more congruently with our own objectives, and how to use them more consciously, skillfully and purposefully, our students will surely benefit. Now that we have explored the power of purposeful suggestion, chapter 11 will set the stage for maximizing the brain's readiness to learn.

Are you ready?

Introspection

What are my own feelings about the topics presented in this chapter? Why do I believe the way I do?

_____

_____

_____

_____

_____

Insights

What are some things I'm discovering now? What's the big picture?

_____

_____

_____

_____

_____

Practical Suggestions

What are the resulting actions that follow from my beliefs? In what ways might I improve?

_____

_____

_____

_____

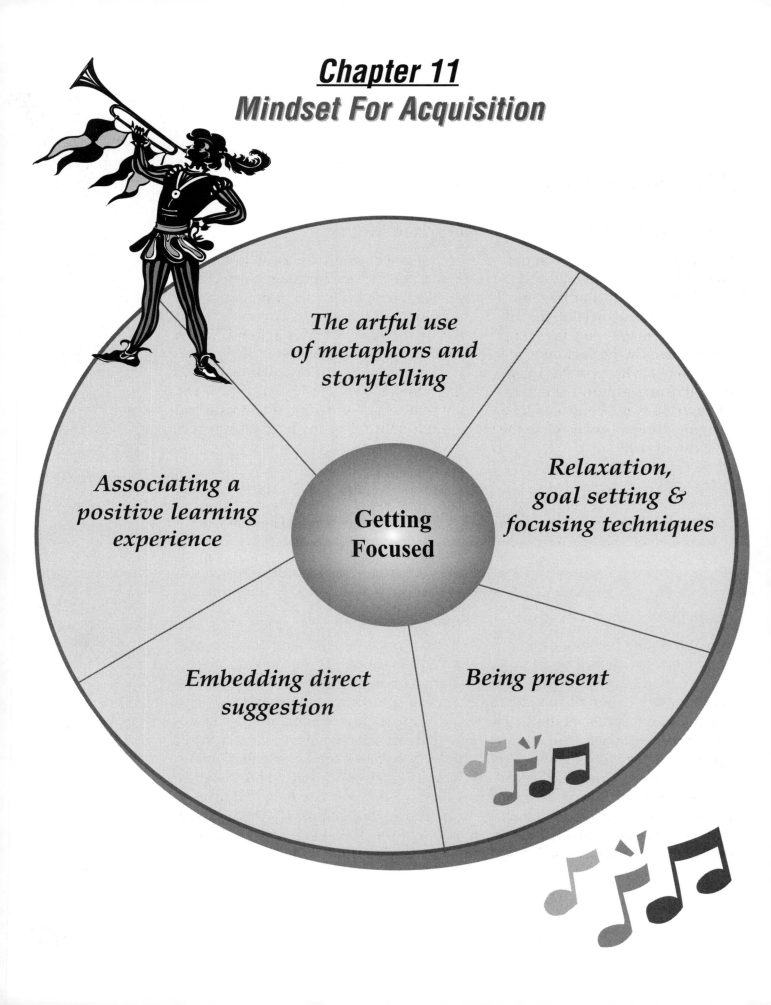

Chapter 11
Mindset For Acquisition

Getting Focused

The artful use of metaphors and storytelling

Relaxation, goal setting & focusing techniques

Being present

Embedding direct suggestion

Associating a positive learning experience

Mindset for Acquisition

Sample Relaxation "Being Present" Exercise

If you make the assumption that your students will come to class in every possible mindset except the one that's perfect for foreign language acquisition, you'll be right most of the time. Because the instructor is such a potent carrier of suggestion, we need to make sure we prepare ourselves and our students for each class - to get calm, present and mentally focused. With this in mind, I often begin classes in the beginning weeks of a course with a guided relaxation or fantasy loaded with positive images and affirmative suggestions. This serves to help the entire group unify for the purpose of being fully ready to learn. Though there are many useful books on the subject of centering, meditation and imaging, (several are listed in the bibliography) the following brief excerpt provides an example of an effective relaxation script:

> *Let's take a moment to center our energies and become fully present. As we allow our breath to become deeper we will experience increasing relaxation and steadiness. With each in-breath, a wave of relaxing, calming energy flows in to quiet any tensions and discomforts. Any thoughts or distracting concerns pass right by, and you feel calmly alert and fully present, ready to experience and respond with your full self.*

Goal-setting and Focusing Techniques

Visual thinking techniques offer a powerful means for achieving our purposes and objectives. Before beginning a new course and at the start of each class, I take a few minutes to sit quietly and rehearse (in my imagination) as vividly as possible how I would like to be in class, what specific things I want to do, and the qualities I want to embody (i.e., caring, support, joy, delight, humor). I visualize myself interacting in specific ways with certain students (i.e., receptively, openly, supportively, firmly). Visual thinking exercises can be extended to students, as well. I frequently lead students in a visualization where they see themselves learning and being the way they would most like to be. Effective at the beginning of class, before a test, or before starting almost any task, visualization techniques always make an impact. The following script offers an example of a visualization I might use at the beginning of a new course:

As you relax, allow your imagination to help you recall a full and satisfying learning experience. It may have occurred recently or long ago, alone or with others - a time when you learned something important. Recall the setting. What do you see? What do you hear? What do you feel? (curiosity? joy? confidence? delight?). Allow yourself to re-experience the qualities, let them fill you. And now, as you gradually shift back to the present moment, allow the positive qualities of your special learning experience to remain alive within you; and to serve as a resource for opening yourself fully to the day before you.

I have learned that the effectiveness of these guided visualizations depends every bit as much on my timing and intonation as on my choice of words. I find it very helpful to become an active listener to myself, becoming at some level a listening participant in the visualization. As I do this I feel much more aligned and congruent with what I am saying. I feel immediately more relaxed myself, and I sense a deepened rapport with my students.

The Artful Use of Metaphors

Metaphors can be a powerful tool in tapping the suggestive power of language. Metaphors and images are the primary communicative means of the subconscious. Using metaphors to respond creatively to problems - in the form of stories, jokes, parables, fairy tales - has been a form favored by teachers since time immemorial. All the major religious traditions have made use of the metaphorical story to communicate their teachings. Metaphors appeal to multiple levels within us simultaneously. They are frequently able to bypass or penetrate the set attitudes, categories and limitations of the conscious mind.

Speaking the language of the subconscious, the metaphorical story can provide parallels to our own life situations as well as universal patterns of behavior, joy, suffering, and conflict. Such parallels often provide resolutions which resonate meaningfully and acceptably with the inner experience and personality structure of the listener. As we learn to communicate more effectively on this level with our students, we can better tap the potential which resides there. Used purposefully, metaphors can greatly assist our students in transforming the beliefs and self-images which may be limiting them. Stories not only entertain, they can facilitate growth and change. The use and/or interpretation of metaphor has become a standard therapeutic strategy for counselors and psychotherapists, and a fine art among the best of them. Carl Jung and Milton Erickson (see bibliography) are just two of the most well-known psychologists who have contributed models for both understanding and working transformationally with symbolic and metaphoric communication.

Metaphors appeal to multiple levels within us simultaneously

Incorporating guided relaxation exercises and imagery experiences into the curriculum is a good way to begin using metaphor for immediate impact. An excellent introduction to therapeutic change through metaphorical story is provided by author David Gordon in *Therapeutic Metaphors* (1978). Two examples of how metaphorical communication are used in the Joyful Fluency classroom follow. But first, a little processing time might help embed what you've read thus far.

Reader's Reflection

In what ways do you currently use metaphor in your teaching?

Recalling A Positive Learning Experience

I use the following combined guided relaxation exercise and guided fantasy on the first day of class to optimally prepare students for joyful fluency:

As you begin to collect your energies and become more and more present, you can notice the regularity of your breathing, allowing it to be as comfortable, slow and deep as feels good. If it feels more comfortable to close your eyes, that is fine. And as you become aware of the chair supporting your body, securely and easily, you can let any discomfort go as if it were flowing right out through the chair. These special chairs have been provided so that it is easy to relax. The support for your head encourages you to relax your neck, your head and your mind. The arm supports allow you to rest your shoulders and open easily to the new experiences before you...

The pleasant colors and objects in the room invite you to enjoy yourself through your senses. And as you relax deeper and deeper, you may find it easy to drift back to a time when you learned something new... when learning filled you with joy and satisfaction... a time when you experienced learning that was as easy and as natural as breathing in ... and breathing out...

This special, positive learning experience may have occurred recently or months or years ago. You may have been alone, with a friend, a teacher, or a guide. And as you re-experience or re-live this special, positive learning experience, you may hear all

Guided fantasies are most effective when they are not overly directive

the sounds that were there... smell the fragrances... see all the details of the scene... feel the positive sensations accompanying the experience. You may even become aware of the essence of the experience that made it so special...

You may be experiencing feelings of wonder, delight, joy, mastery, self-appreciation, excitement, confidence, or another quality. Whatever that essence is, you will be able to let it begin filling you now... so that the essence of this special learning experience resonates throughout your being... reminding you that this special, positive learning experience is a resource for you... a valuable possession which you can call upon to remind you how you love to learn... how you are able to learn naturally, easily and successfully...

You may even realize that as you embark upon new learning experiences that all you have to do is to recall your positive learning experience, and your mind will become attuned to the way you like to learn... to the way you learn most effectively and successfully. And in the days and weeks ahead, as we help each other enjoy learning together, you may find that there is some part of you, some inner sign which awakens when it is reminded of your special experience... And you may find that this special essence will begin to emerge again and again to help you experience the kind of learning you are seeking...

In a minute we will begin returning with our conscious awareness to the moment, to this room... And when we do, you will find it easy to bring with you some of the essence of your special, positive learning... You will feel refreshed, alert, and awake... ready to utilize your inner resources and the resources of the group and this class to full advantage. Now, in your own time, at your own pace, slowly bring your awareness back here, to this room, together with the other people here. As you open your eyes, notice the objects and people around you. Listen to the sounds in the room. Feel the firm floor beneath your feet. Welcome back. I sense that this was a special experience for some of you. I trust that it provided us a positive way to begin our learning adventure together.

Commentary on Guided Relaxations

The tempo is slow, steady and relaxed. The conscious mind tends to be in a hurry. It may well become bored with the fantasy. That is fine. The subconscious mind is the one we are primarily speaking to here. Speak with rhythmical pauses. This can assist in the deepening of the relaxation process. Students' breathing will tend to synchronize to the rhythmical delivery.

How direct or indirect should the message be? When facilitating guided fantasies such as the one above, much of the metaphorical or imagery content will be provided by the student. In general, guided fantasies are most effective when they are not overly directive. The details, when left to the listener to provide, will generally be more powerful. An exception to this is when you are using guided fantasies to review language content. In such a case, the teacher provides a wealth of detail and vocabulary woven together with interesting images.

One of the most powerful suggestive tools of linguistic communication is the use of embedded suggestions. Few people enjoy being told what to do. In fact many individuals react negatively to overt authority and have developed a kind of reflex resistance to verbal commands. Embedding suggestions within certain linguistic structures is an effective way to circumvent resistance to positive suggestions intended to help students successfully access their own learning potential. Used in such a way, positive suggestive images can bypass the conscious mind, eluding detection by resistance mechanisms. More than 20 such suggestions are contained in the above guided fantasy.

Reader's Reflection

How have you used suggestion in the past? How can you use more of it in the future?

How to Embed Direct Suggestions

Through subtle changes in pitch, intonation, or directional projection, it is possible to "mark" suggestions in such a way that they are consistently communicated in a characteristic way, but unnoticed by the conscious mind. Another suggestive technique used in this fantasy is the embedding of direct suggestions: i.e., "... when learning filled you with joy and satisfaction ... " or "... a time when you experienced that learning is easy and as natural as breathing in and out ..." Notice that this second example abruptly changes verb tense from past to present serving to intensify the experience and draw the listener more deeply into the immediacy of the moment.

Experience builds confidence & with each successful step it becomes easier to stretch ourselves toward the growth we seek

Another association strategy called anchoring is used extensively by therapists, entertainers and marketing experts to further embed suggestions. An anchor is any stimulus that evokes a consistent response pattern from a person. Does the name Pavlov ring a bell? Any sensory modality may be used, but in a teaching context, auditory/verbal anchors are most practical. In the above guided fantasy, for example, the teacher might consistently "mark" out the words "special, positive learning experience" with a perceptible shift in intonation. It is important to use an intonation which is distinctly different from the one normally used in regular speaking as indiscriminate word choices can weaken the continuing associational strength of the anchor. In using the anchoring technique, I try to synchronize the first anchor intonation to the moment when the most students are recalling their positive learning experience. I reinforce the association several times more during the recall experience. If the timing is good so that the anchoring association coincides with the fully evoked experience, the anchor will "take," and the next time the anchor/stimulus is used the associated experience will be accessed. Thus, the stimulus/response mechanism can be called upon to serve the learning process on later occasions.

The first week of the course provides a valuable opportunity to root as deeply as possible, the students' positive associations to new language learning. Having anchored on the first day the experience of a highly positive learning experience in the student's past, I evoke the essence of that experience by using the phrase "special, positive learning experience" with the same perceivable intonation I used to mark it during the guided fantasy on the first day - without having to repeat the entire process. I might begin the second or third day with a short relaxation exercise before commencing some communicative activities. For example, I might say:

"And as you continue to relax, you may begin to look forward to the special ... positive ... learning experiences ahead... " Effective anchoring requires practice and consistency. I have found it helpful to begin using the technique modestly, perhaps, marking a phrase one day, making a note of it, and then repeating it in a purposeful context with the same intonation for several days thereafter. Experience builds confidence and with each successful step it becomes easier to stretch ourselves toward the growth we seek.

Summary

In this chapter we explored techniques for evoking a positive state of mind so important to the process of foreign language acquisition. We experienced a sample guided relaxation and fantasy exercise used frequently at the start of a JoF course. We discussed how metaphors impact the subconscious mind; and how to use direct suggestion as a means for accessing a student's full potential. Chapter 12, The Magic of Metaphors, will explore the mechanics of using metaphor in story form; and will provide a powerful example of its use in the JoF classroom. ***Let the story begin!***

Introspection

What are my own feelings about the topics presented in this chapter? Why do I believe the way I do?

_____

_____

_____

_____

_____

Insights

What are some things I'm discovering now? What's the big picture?

_____

_____

_____

_____

_____

Practical Suggestions

What are the resulting actions that follow from my beliefs? In what ways might I improve?

_____

_____

_____

_____

_____

Chapter 12
The Magic of Metaphors

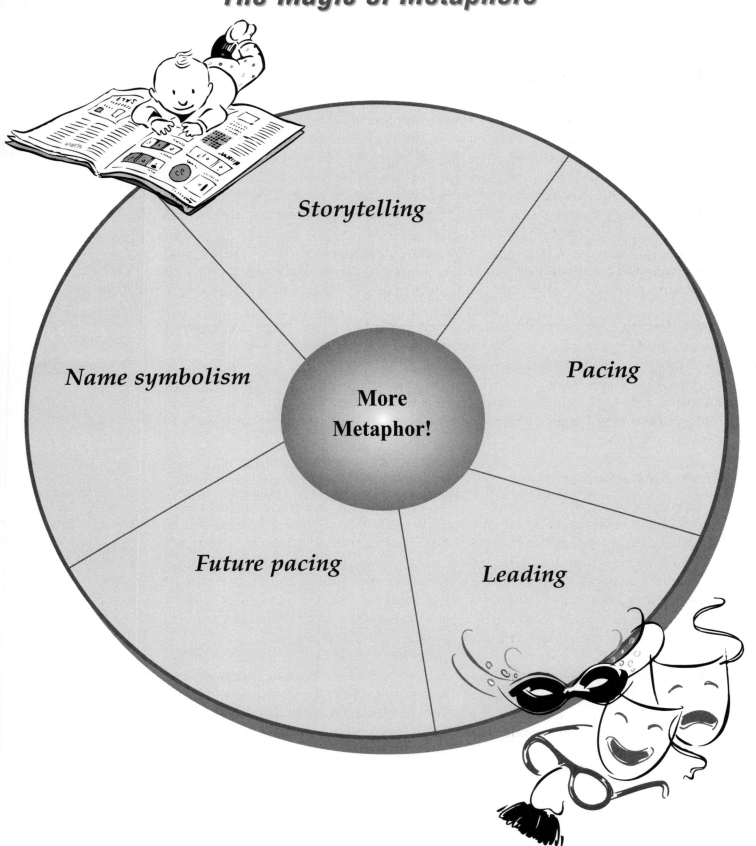

Storytelling

Pacing

More Metaphor!

Name symbolism

Future pacing

Leading

The Magic of Metaphors

Metaphor has been used in the practice of teaching and learning for ions. Everywhere you look metaphors make suggestions that you may or may not be aware of on a conscious level. When used in story form, metaphor creates an anthropological and social affinity for human drama. Shakespeare was an expert in its use. Notice too how most television programs, from cartoons, sports broadcasts, and soap operas to news casts, infomercials and gossip shows, present information in story form. Metaphor instills the learning of content or process on a very subtle, often subconscious level. When the subconscious is activated or accessed, the material enters the mind with no resistance. As a result, metaphors can affect dramatic change in an individual.

The following is an example of the use of metaphor in the language learning classroom. It is a story I tell in my beginning German language class. It can be used more than once in a course. For example, I might tell the story in English during the first few days of class. Later, I retell it in the target language. The first telling is meant to reinforce rapport and build confidence early on. The re-telling in the new language helps students bridge their learning - from past to present to future. The story goes like this:

Story As Metaphor

This is the story of a young woman, Christina, who leaves the home of her parents in order to make her own way in the world. She is seeking to go beyond the ever-familiar routine of her family and take on the challenge of the new and unfamiliar. Thus, she travels to the UniCenter of Growth and Wisdom, a special place cherished by seekers of all kinds, located in the heart of the land known as Namreg. She arrives in the fall, just as the leaves are beginning to change to colors of deep red, orange and yellow, and the trees, themselves, are turning within for the winter.

Christina is somewhat anxious because she has never been to Namreg and does not understand the language spoken there. When she arrives and hears people speaking so rapidly in such foreign ways, she feels afraid and wonders if she might have made a mistake in leaving home. It was so easy to understand her friends there. Many learners reside at the UniCenter besides herself, and she thinks they don't appear to be afraid.

Everywhere
you look,
metaphors
make sugges-
tions that you
may or may
not be aware of
on a conscious
level

Caught up in her feelings of doubt, Christina walks around aimlessly until she meets one of the welcome guides who helps "new seekers" begin their course of initiation at the UniCenter. The guide's name is Karelov. Karelov is a kind, gentle man who greets her in her own language, and yet soon has her feeling comfortable listening to his native Namreg. She is amazed at how relaxed and confident she feels with her guide. Her understanding of what he tells her grows quickly, and before long she is beginning to respond back in Namreg. Karelov recognizes that Christina has all the abilities she needs to thrive in Namreg.

With Karelov's insight, support and encouragement Christina begins to open her mind and heart to the opportunities around her. Karelov spends many hours with Christina and a small group of seekers. He tells many stories. He plays delightful and fascinating games with them; and listens with patience and interest. They all learn rapidly, scarcely realizing it is happening. Christina's confidence grows quickly. She begins to speak to other seekers, to laugh, play, and joke with them. She looks forward to their sessions together. She recognizes that their challenges, fears, strengths, and hopes are similar to her own; and the warm bonds of friendship begin to deepen.

One of these friends, Bruno, invites her to the annual festival dance in Namreg. Karelov has taught them the traditional dance forms of Namreg, and they demonstrate their skills with ease and delight at the festival occasion. There are not many seekers at the dance who are as inexperienced as Christina and Bruno; and many of the natives come to them and congratulate them on their naturalness and ease in expressing themselves in such new forms.

During one of the intermissions, one of the traditional dance instructors of the town by the name of Pedantaway asks them how many hours and days they must have drilled for such a performance. How surprised he is when they respond that they have never drilled, but just danced for fun to Karelov's music and imaginative descriptions. The dance instructor cannot believe it and suspects they must be lying. Christina and Bruno become a little confused and wonder if they did something wrong. They cannot understand all this fuss, all these questions, all this analysis of their learning which had just happened so naturally.

Just at this moment, Karelov and his partner, Bellissa, who are also attending the dance, gracefully come up to Christina and Bruno and invite them to join in a dance for four. The young pair tell Karelov of the incident with the dance instructor, and Karelov smiles. He explains that, "the UniCenter is not free of those who get stuck in outworn beliefs about how learning must occur. Many still cannot accept that mastery can come without strenuous, forced effort. Pedantaway, it seems, has forgotten that play and natural spontaneity release our best capacities to learn." Christina and Bruno realize from their own recent experiences that what Karelov is saying is true. As the kind teacher offers his hands for another round of the dance, a smile of recognition appears on the young couple's faces. In an instant, they are all again dancing freely and naturally, and with skill and delight.

The next day Karelov announces to Christina, Bruno and the rest of the group that their initiation orientation is complete. They have all mastered naturally and with ease a basic understanding of and competence level at speaking Namreg. They are ready to proceed on their continuing quest. Their understanding and vision of themselves and others has grown, as has their confidence and self-appreciation. The friendships will continue, the pleasant memories will remain, and the ending is but a beginning. As Karelov concludes his remarks, he opens his arms, inviting all the group to join him in the great circle dance of strength and unity.

Christina has since become a fine teacher herself. Bruno has become a master of Namreg communication. They and their friends continue their quests, without haste, following easily and naturally the best guide of all - the Karelov who resides within them.

Reader's Reflection

What metaphors do you identify in the above example? How might they impact the learner?

Commentary

The purpose of the above story is to provide students with a positive, supportive metaphor for their own experience as learners. The metaphorical quality of this story is rather obvious and would probably be perceived consciously by some students. This is not necessarily good or bad. However, for students who are resistant to learning, the more subtle and indirect the metaphor, the more likely its acceptance. For the fearful student who is probably lacking confidence, such a story can be effective on both the conscious and unconscious levels.

The best constructed metaphor is isomorphic (or structurally parallel) to the learner's situation. When working with one individual it is easier, of course, to tailor the metaphor. Working with groups calls for a more general metaphorical approach, but still one that fits the general type of group situation or group personality. The following assumptions based on situational elements that characterize the typical JoF student were made in the above example:

- Students' past experiences have highly conditioned their attitudes, behaviors and responses. They are partly aware of this, partly not.

- Coming to the university and to a JoF class is on some level connected to the student's deeper personal quest toward meaning, success, and fulfillment.

- The challenge of learning a new language (perhaps even of attending the university) is anxiety-producing. There will be feelings of doubt and of "I can't."

- A good guide/teacher can provide an environment where students' fears will disappear and their natural abilities will be affirmed and fostered.

- Students will encounter teachers and others who will insist on the prevailing socio-cultural norm that learning is difficult and requires strenuous conscious effort.

While our story example acknowledges the above factors or assumptions (a method known as pacing), the following suggestive elements were built into the metaphor to suggest alternatives and possible resolutions:

Pacing

Pacing describes the variety of things one can do to acknowledge another person's situation. Whether it's a response of "I hear you" or "I understand" or "I see", communication is only completely effective when we actually do hear the person speaking. Pacing can be an effective means for establishing rapport. In the above story the entire first paragraph has a pacing function. It is designed to mirror metaphorically the general situation of most students in the beginning JoF class.

The best constructed metaphor is isomorphic to the learner's situation

122

Leading

Once rapport is established with the students, the next step is to initiate movement towards the desired state for learning. In our story this function is embodied by the guide Karelov. He meets the students where they are and gently guides them away from their doubts and fears toward an appreciation of their natural learning capacities and goals. Karelov is a metaphor for the ideal teacher. The following examples represent other suggestive elements in our story:

- In the third and fourth paragraphs, words like confidence, ease, opening up, naturalness, success, play, and enjoyment dominate the descriptions. This vocabulary reflects positively suggestive language and images.

- Paragraphs four and eight give expression to the positive effects of supportive group interaction and inter-personal bonding. Positive group dynamics is an essential ingredient for the success of a JoF class.

- Paragraphs six and seven represent the student's overcoming of renewed doubt. Students who learn through an acquisition approach rather than a conscious learning approach may question their own learning process or be questioned by others who are suspect of the new approach.

The challenge in the above story is presented in the form of a pedantic dance instructor who needs to explain Christina's and Bruno's learning in conscious, analytical terms. Students with acquired competence aren't likely prepared to defend or explain the pedagogical approach involved in their learning. This story offers the authority of the guide/teacher as a means for ensuring the learner's confidence when faced with inner and/or outer challenges.

Future Pacing

This strategy involves bridging to the future. Once the problem state (such as tedious learning) has been successfully overcome through the use of metaphors, then the story suggests images of possible successful future applications or expressions. In our story, for example, the career manifestations of Christina and Bruno and the continuing growth of the group as a whole, offer positive and plausible results with which the student may choose to identify.

When the subconscious is activated or accessed, the material enters the mind with no resistance

Name Symbolism:

- **Karelov is a play on the words care and love**
- **Namreg is German in reverse**
- **Pedantaway is a play on words: away with pedants**
- **Christina and Bruno are typical German names; and easy for beginning students to identify with**
- **UniCenter is a play on University**

Summary

Pacing establishes rapport with the listener's present state. Leading involves transformational work, in this case, using a metaphorical story to mirror a transformational growth process with a desired outcome. Future pacing bridges the inner (transformational) experiences to possible expressions in the external world. In addition, the story provides abundant opportunities for embedding positive suggestions, suggestive play on words, and evocative imagery. The entire process is designed to appeal to the subconscious mind, and to access its potential for acquisition of a new communication system. Metaphors are not the *only*, or the single *best*, way to encourage second language acquisition, but they provide powerful support for the process. In the next chapter we will explore the topic of active learning and how this methodology relates to the phases of information engagement, retrieval and usage. *Joyful Fluency is within sight!*

For students who are resistant to learning, the more subtle and indirect the metaphor, the more likely its acceptance

Introspection

What are my own feelings about the topics presented in this chapter? Why do I believe the way I do?

_____

_____

_____

_____

_____

Insights

What are some things I'm discovering now? What's the big picture?

_____

_____

_____

_____

_____

Practical Suggestions

What are the resulting actions that follow from my beliefs? In what ways might I improve?

_____

_____

_____

_____

_____

Chapter 13
Active Learning:
Engagement, Retrieval, & Usage

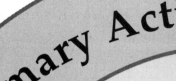

Primary Activation Activities

- Puppets
- Costume props
- Comprehension check
- Whole group choral

- Echo antics
- Simultaneous role reading
- Individual or small group reading

Activating Learning... The "Snowball Effect"

Secondary Activation Activities

- Ball toss
- Puppets
- Desire to speak
- Dramatizations

- Novel objects
- Pictures, slides, video tapes
- Card games

- Appeal to imagination
- Guided fantasy
- Props
- Singing & dancing

Active Learning: Engagement, Retrieval, and Usage

Most second language teachers delight in the first moments when students begin to actively use the target language. Activation begins as students truly listen and comprehend, or as they grasp the relation between a facial expression, body gesture, picture, voice intonation and language meaning. They constantly demonstrate their active comprehension when they correctly respond to commands and requests, nod in agreement or disagreement, or display congruent facial expressions.

Activation also means beginning to use expressively the speech patterns which have been heard, internalized, sorted, patterned, and associated. A guiding principle is: Don't push students to speak! Stated positively, we would say, "Our goal is spontaneous speaking, not forced activation." A great deal of your homework as a facilitator has to do with creating the threat-free immersion environment in which the input is high and attitude is playful. Once that step has been completed, the next step is to begin the process of receptively and expressively activating the previously encoded material. This involves finding the means to facilitate retrieval and natural ease in use. The activation phase includes two main stages - primary and secondary which are described in this chapter:

Setting the Stage for Easy Activation

The primary activation session begins with the class following the concert presentations. This is the students' first expressive engagement with the material. Before beginning this phase I always spend time reinforcing positive group rapport by sharing humorous anecdotes, listening to a short song or poem, or most often, a visit by, of all things, a puppet.

When I first considered using puppets in class, I was afraid my students would think it was silly or feel insulted. I had no experience in the puppet department, but having watched a mentor use this approach successfully, I decided to take the risk. Soon after venturing into this unfamiliar territory, I became a big advocate of puppet aides in language learning. Now I always introduce "Onkel Fritz" after the first three to six hours of each course. By this time group cohesiveness has usually been achieved and students are delighted to find that learning doesn't have to be all serious work. Onkel Fritz provides many opportunities for the class to experience spontaneous "happenings" in the realm of fantasy.

As with students' acceptance of fantasy identities, their assent to interact with a puppet is a step towards the atmosphere of "play" that is all important to the JoF classroom. Communication is generally conducted more freely with a humorous character than with a "real" person, especially when the real person happens to be the teacher. By nature, a puppet represents a character of the imagination and is generally associated with fun; thus, making it an excellent role-model for relaxed expression.

Puppet Possibilities

With the assent to play comes spontaneity & a sense of openness - the optimal climate for language acquisition & learning in general

With the assent to play comes spontaneity and a sense of openness - the optimal climate for language acquisition and learning in general. My primary puppet, Onkel Fritz, quickly becomes a family member of the class, and interaction with him (all in German, of course) becomes the springboard for some especially effective communication activities. Onkel Fritz is a balding, 70-year-old Bavarian adventurer, who loves Schnapps and females and is convinced that he is as young (at heart) as anyone. His engaging and humorous anecdotes and appeals for opinions and advice rapidly lay the groundwork for colorful personal relationships with nearly everyone in the class. His flirtatious bent produces an amazing variety of responses, from motherly reprimands and advice to brotherly alliances. One class consented to help him find a more permanent female partner, offered strategies, and suggested wording for a personal ad in the classifieds. Several days later a letter for him had been pushed under the door before class - from "Brunhilde", a new female admirer who was inspired by his romantic ad.

Variations on puppet interactions are limited only by our imaginations. I have observed that imaginations, both mine and my students', seem to expand as steadily as communication competence does in a climate of playful risk-taking. Puppets stimulate the imaginative child in both students and teachers. This dimension, when purposefully integrated into our classes, can enhance learning dramatically.

Primary Activation Activities

Though puppets are used most during the "secondary activation" phase discussed later, and in setting the stage as described above, they are also highly effective in staging the "primary activation" of material. Once a light and comfortable atmosphere has been established, I move into playful engagement with the material from the previous sessions concert presentations. I typically use several of the following strategies for primary activation: 1) whole group choral echo/antics; 2) simultaneous role reading in dyads or triads; 3) individual or small group role reading for the class with costume props; and 4) comprehension check. These activities are used for a block of text approximately 250 words in length.

Whole Group Choral Echo/Antics

This is generally the first activity I conduct when introducing new textual material. I ask the group to stand with their texts in hand and echo my model reading. Standing up permits students more physical involvement and also facilitates fuller voice production. I urge them to echo and even exaggerate my dramatic intonation, to be loud and boisterous, and above all, to be expressive! I emphasize that the focus is on playful, enjoyable interaction; and ask them to use the images in the text as they speak to find accompanying gestures with their hands, arms, heads or bodies. I explain that by simultaneously and actively using our imaginations, the sound of our voices, the gestures of our bodies and an emotionally playful spirit, we are maximizing a range of learning styles and memory anchors. Such an explanation seems to help students more fully engage in the activity.

Role Reading in Dyads or Triads

I usually follow the above whole group choral work with a variation on the same material in dyads or triads depending on the number of roles in that particular section of the text. Note that since the primary text is written as a drama in dialogue form, there are always character roles to interpret playfully and imaginatively. My instructions are to re-enact the dialogue section as freely, expressively, and dramatically as possible. I ask students to stand for this activity so that they can move freely as the action in the text calls for it.

Role Reading for the Class with Costume Props

After the above energetic, playful and enjoyable engagement with the text, I often ask for volunteers to enact the reading for the whole class. By this point students are usually so warmed up that there are always volunteers. The presentation can be conducted by any number of students in the group. It is important to keep this activity playful and light. Costume props in this exercise help keep the focus off the "real" personality of the reader. Hats of all kinds, glasses, jewelry, jackets, aprons, etc. make useful props, many of them brought in by students themselves.

The teacher's corrections are minimal at this point, and are designed to serve as encouragement rather than as a critical standard. The focus remains on the delight of dramatic play, not on the reading exercise. Students ought to have the feeling that they are doing this with each other, not for the teacher. With supportive encouragement, students quickly realize that they are able to create widely varying shades of expression. This is found entertaining by their classmates - a reward far more appreciated than a grade from the teacher. A hearty round of applause at the conclusion of the enactment caps the playful performance.

Costume props help keep the focus off the "real" personality of the reader

Can you think of other strategies that might be useful in the primary activation stage?

Comprehension Check

The next step is a comprehension check which serves to consolidate students' growing understanding. This activity, like the others, is designed to avoid an exercise-like feeling. Thus, I begin expressively rephrasing the key lines of the act, pausing to inquire in an interested tone of voice: "What does that mean in English?" Students answer as a group; they are not called on to answer individually.

Occasionally one or two students will begin to dominate the responses by answering before everyone else. Rather than asking them to withhold their responses and thereby turning them "off," I quietly acknowledge their contribution with my facial expression and continue asking, both verbally and with my eyes, for the answer again from a different part of the room. The message is subtle, yet effective. The quick responders begin pacing their responses with the rest of the group. The slower responders see that they will be waited for and are valued. As a result, the class does not develop that common split between those who contribute and those who don't. I avoid allowing this activity to become tedious by keeping my own curiosity and interest level high, and by timing the activity according to the engagement level of the group. I end the activity by generously acknowledging their achievement.

Secondary Activation Activities

In the early stages of a JoF course (0-20 hours), the teacher is the major source of "comprehensible input" through considerable elaborate talking. This allows students to experience their ability to comprehend a new language. Production is not demanded, only invited, so as to maintain a low anxiety level. Although students do read material aloud in the primary activation phase, the emphasis is on comprehension. This approach shares the premise of Asher, Krashen, Terrell, and others that comprehension precedes production.

As students' comprehension grows and confidence naturally builds, the desire to speak is automatic. Encouraging the natural desire to speak by providing real opportunities for communication, rather than word drills, is the goal of the secondary activation phase. This phase is characterized by playful, imaginative, spontaneous ways of encouraging full and authentic receptive and expressive communication.

The primary activation phase is, as the name implies, the first activation of the newly introduced textual material. These activities, as described in the preceding section, stay quite close to a line-by-line engagement with the text. The secondary activation phase does not attempt to stay so close to the text. The activities of this phase, described below, include freer variations on the text, picking out idiomatic, syntactical, grammatical constructions and lexical groups for imaginative, playful elaboration. The student may not be consciously aware of the structural focus. His/her attention is directed to the communicative opportunities. The strategies and activities I have found most effective for the secondary activation phase are described below:

Appeal to the Imagination

One of the most powerful ways to tap into the resources of the imagination is to involve students in their own fantasy identity change. This simple device can be very powerful, encouraging abandonment to a less defensive, more playful and relaxed atmosphere. Simply greeting a student with their fantasy name at the beginning of class usually serves to activate the "anchored" positive associations with the identity change. Continuing to chat with them as if the fiction were real will most often spark an outpouring of unselfconscious imaginative sharing.

I may ask what "Heinrich" was up to last night, spotlighting in a gentle way the opportunities for humorous amplification. I usually attempt to link his "story" with the imaginary stories of others in the class so that quickly and easily a web of personal interaction is generated. This is an easy and highly effective way to set a positive, upbeat, and productive tone at the start of a class.

Guided fantasy in the target language is another very effective tool for elaboration and confidence building. I often use a relaxation fantasy combined with an imaginative guided journey that contains content and vocabulary elements from the previous class for review purposes. This also provides another opportunity for embedding positive suggestions that may enhance a student's self-concept. For example, suggest that the student see him/herself interacting in the target language with full confidence and ease, perhaps speaking to one of the engaging characters in the text.

Using Props

Props of all kinds tie into and enhance most activities used in the active learning phase. Some of the most obvious props are described on the next page:

Encouraging the natural desire to speak by providing real opportunities for communication is the goal of the secondary activation phase

Costume Articles

Costume Articles

Costumes can instantly transform a person into a playful mood. Hats, jackets, scarves, uniforms, jewelry, etc., all help support an atmosphere of relaxed communication.

Novel Physical Objects

Physical objects that can be touched, held, smelled, tasted, moved, passed around, etc. spark interest and conversation. They are especially useful during the early stages when more Total Physical Response activities are suggested.

Pictures, Slides, and Videotapes

Visuals provide the stimulus for great quantities of comprehensible input and spoken exchange. Basic equipment for you is your "picture file" which can be enhanced with photos from magazines. Numerous images from many angles of reality provide a rich context and stimulate student reaction. Videotapes and slides offer additional visual resources for orchestrated immersion possibilities.

Puppets

As discussed at the beginning of this chapter, puppets provide one of the most productive means for creating a conducive climate for language acquisition.

Singing, Miming, and Dancing

Music, movement, and speech mutually reinforce each other and experientially deepen the learning process. When students see that singing, gesturing, and dancing can be safe and fun they embrace it with gusto. In conducting these activities, I have found that students feel safer when they use their fantasy identities. Calling upon "Udo" rather than "Jim" to lead the group in a rousing chorus is seldom perceived as threatening to the student, but rather a harmless way to try something new and potentially fun. I also find that students love to sing folk songs; and a song can be the perfect energy lifter. Before providing a class break, I like to close on an upbeat note so that students leave their seats filled with positive associations. Singing a song serves this purpose well. Due to my own shyness and lack of experience, folk dancing is something I only recently started doing. Once again, I wish I hadn't waited so long. Students love it.

Folk dances are wonderful activities for group bonding and trust building; and they offer a safe and entertaining way to make mistakes, laugh, make physical contact and feel vulnerable collectively - and, to raise group energy dramatically! Some teachers might worry that they are wasting valuable

Communication is generally conducted more freely with a humorous character than with a real person, especially when the "real" person happens to be the teacher

teaching time on "non-verbal" activities. Remember though that students will be interacting spontaneously in the target language; and that dancing allows cultural flavors to penetrate the student at a cellular level.

Dramatizations

Basic to the JoF approach is dramatizing language material in interesting and humorous skits. Using this technique students move naturally out of the early phases which focus on listening comprehension into speech production. Playful, dramatic contexts are very helpful in the transition to speech production because they provide students with an opportunity to use extensive non-verbal contextual cues in the communication process. Even in the first weeks, complex communicative interactions are possible without requiring substantial expressive speech. The more communication success a student experiences early on, the greater chance s/he will continue to take the necessary risks involved in learning a new language.

Short skits that simulate such experiences as finding a seat on a bus, checking in at a hotel, ordering a meal, or going through customs are activities used by many language teachers. It is not the activity per se, but the joyful atmosphere in which these activities occur that personifies the JoF classroom. Once students have truly assented to participate in a positively contagious environment, almost any activity can succeed. Where everyone is wanting and expecting success, there will be success.

Reader's Reflection

What strategies have you used that would reinforce material in the secondary activation phase?

Ball Toss Game

As previously discussed, in an atmosphere of play, the conscious focus is not upon the students' intentional linguistic performance. Thus, students begin to use vocabulary and language structures almost without realizing it. "Playing ball," provides a favorite example. The teacher tosses a large, easy-to-catch ball to a student as s/he asks, for example, "How are you, today?" The student answers while tossing back the ball. The immediate, conscious focus is on catching and throwing the ball, offsetting any strained, expectant attention on language production. If the student is hesitant and experiences difficulty, the ball throwing continues while the teacher rephrases the question in such a way as to facilitate success, perhaps, offering several choices, such as "great," "so/so," "fantastic."

Card Games

Card games can be very effective since much comprehensible input can be generated by all during the interplay. "Strip-21" (a variation on Blackjack), is a favorite card game of students. In Strip-21, students "bet" with a piece of clothing (a shoe, earring, sweater, etc. - or borrow one, if they are already down to basics). As they place their bet, they name the object and place it in the center. As cards are turned up, they are named, and the number combinations are counted. The play is usually accompanied by related talk, the spirit is fun, and the language is usually rich and varied.

Again, the effectiveness of these and other games derives less from the specific nature of the activity than from the skillfully created and guided atmosphere in which they occur. Although the bulk of new vocabulary is presented in the concert sessions, the activation phases continue to offer new input, both in the form of supplementary elaboration and usage skills. Through authentic communication experiences students learn intonation, cadence, timing, and body language. This new input, when authentic, is essential to true communicative competence. Often neglected in traditional language learning approaches, authentic communication opportunities underscore the difference between life-like and lifeless learning situations.

The Snowball Effect

There is an accelerative "snow-ball effect" when students are succeeding and enjoying themselves. The operating expectation becomes that of success. Risk-taking increases, for it does not lead to "failure" but only to helpful, supportive feedback designed to facilitate more success. In a climate of mutual support, mistakes may elicit "laughter with," but ought never include "laughing at." The behavioral model of the instructor is crucial in establishing positive group dynamics. His/her authoritative presence lends support to what's positive and ignores that which is negative. An adage I have found useful is: Whatever we attend to with care - be it opportunities or problems - will grow proportionately.

Summary

In sum, the purpose of the activation phases is to assist students in bringing to life the material they received and encoded during the musical presentations. This is most effectively accomplished without drilling, through activities which playfully stimulate the imagination. A prerequisite for success is a safe and supportive atmosphere which encourages spontaneity and risk-taking. In chapter 14, we will examine the implications of error correction, grammar acquisition, and homework. **Success and enjoyment go hand-in-hand!**

There is an accelerative "snow-ball effect" when students are succeeding & enjoying themselves

Introspection

What are my own feelings about the topics presented in this chapter? Why do I believe the way I do?

_____

_____

_____

_____

_____

Insights

What are some things I'm discovering now? What's the big picture?

_____

_____

_____

_____

_____

Practical Suggestions

What are the resulting actions that follow from my beliefs? In what ways might I improve?

_____

_____

_____

_____

_____

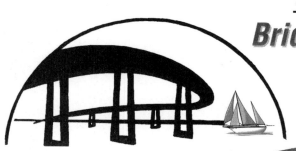

Chapter 14
Bridge to Fluency

Language Competence is Achieved Effortlessly & Joyfully!

Grammar:

- *Natural acquisition*
- *Balance of learning and acquisition strategies*

Error Correction:

- *Echo technique*
- *Minimize direct correction*
- *Stimulate student confidence*
- *Error ossification*
- *Experimentation*
- *Real Competency*

Homework:

- *Not always compatible with acquisition techniques*
- *Listening to tapes is good*
- *Reading over dialogue is good*

Bridge To Fluency

As you may recall from chapter two, Tracy Terrell (The Natural Approach Model), suggests that language acquisition happens in natural stages: comprehension, early speech, and speech emergence. The preceding chapters were designed to provide the JoF teacher with the materials and tools necessary to build a strong foundation upon which the Joyful Fluency classroom can be facilitated. Such a classroom will provide students with maximum support for moving through these natural stages. This concluding chapter examines three related factors: Error Correction, Grammar, and Homework. Depending on how these elements are handled, they can either enhance or detract from the Joyful Fluency process.

The JoF Approach to Error Correction

Teachers are typically trained to judge the "progress" of their students' learning and to grade them accordingly. The JoF Model, however, suggests a different approach. Like other acquisition-focused strategies, JoF minimizes direct correction of student's speech errors. Just as parents do not insist on error-free production when their children begin to verbalize, the brain-compatible teacher rather shows delight and affirmation at all speaking attempts. When language communication begins to emerge, I sometimes gently "echo" a student's attempt using the correct pronunciation so that they receive both an affirmation and a correct model simultaneously. The purpose of this echoing technique is not so much to correct the error, but to stimulate student confidence. The teacher may expand or softly rephrase student output in a way that demonstrates a meaningful conversation. Thus, teacher "intervention" serves to enhance the flow of communication rather than judge the correctness of it.

The objection one most often hears is that without prompt and regular correction students will learn and continually practice incorrect forms, and errors will soon become a fixed pattern. Indeed, error "ossification" is a phenomenon one can witness in many individuals attempting to speak a foreign language. A very common example is that of the American soldier returning from an assignment in Germany who has learned some primitive "street German" and speaks it with deceptive "fluency." That is, the German flows, but its quality is sub-standard, and the soldier may have little or no success in changing these patterns even with much effort.

I believe, however, that a well-orchestrated language acquisition environment avoids many of the factors which most often produce error ossification. In my view, most native speaking environments are very anxiety producing for beginners learning a language. The learner may experience the environment as "threatening," and, therefore, do a brain downshift into more primitive survival strategies. The pressure in a native speaking environment is frequently serious - survival tasks must be negotiated. Survival comes first, sophistication later.

Sophistication, however, is a quality which develops in an atmosphere where there is room for play and experimentation. One must feel relaxed in order to engage in experimentation. Native speaking environments do not often offer such relaxed settings. I believe that all students naturally wish to speak correctly. If, however, students are placed in a situation where they are forced to speak, and feel that they must come up with enough language to "survive," they may grasp any form that seems to work, however primitive, and hang onto it for dear life.

By contrast, when students are invited to speak in a playful context where ego-investment is minimal, they demonstrate a willingness to experiment, take risks and abandon old patterns. When the anxiety level is low in the learning environment, there is less clutching to primitive, error-ridden communicative strategies. A natural urge to try something new emerges, not unlike a small child who experiments or plays with many possible ways to manipulate a toy.

And just as language acquisition occurs unconsciously in most children, the "pattern-maker" within the brain draws inferences and learns language rules gradually and naturally. Relaxed and receptive students in touch with abundant, redundant, yet authentic and "correct" language with little attention given to mistakes will achieve competency. The key here is that if real competency is the goal, you'll have to make risk-taking, joy, and participation higher values than correctness. The wonderful irony is that by making accuracy secondary, you'll end up with greater language competency, and it will be imbued with the love of learning.

The JoF Approach to Grammar

Without taking a radical, "anti-grammar" position, the JoF approach seeks communicative competence through a balance of "learning" and "acquisition" strategies. In fundamental agreement with the work of Stephen Krashen and Tracy Terrell (discussed in chapter two), the JoF Model advocates less formal attention to the conscious teaching of grammatical concepts than other language approaches. The premise that vocabulary development is more important than structural accuracy does not mean that vocabulary will be

Relaxed & receptive students in touch with abundant, redundant, yet authentic & "correct" language with little attention given to mistakes will achieve competency

learned at the expense of grammar. Rather, this approach embraces the belief that once imbued with the ability to speak the target language, students will naturally progress towards correct grammatical usage.

Many teachers want students to learn and apply grammatical rules at the same pace as they learn vocabulary. My own experience bears out Krashen's assertion quoted below that the conscious study of grammar has only minimal, short-term value in the acquisition process.

As Krashen states, "In embracing a communication philosophy, we are not rejecting the idea that students need to acquire (and in some cases learn) a great deal of grammar. In fact, our experience is that they will acquire more grammar this way. Stated simply, focusing on communication goals provides far more comprehensible, meaningful input and encourages more language acquisition than basing the course on grammar. If we provide discussion, hence, input, over a wide variety of topics while pursuing communicative goals, the necessary grammatical structures are automatically provided in the input."

This is not to say, however, that students should not be assigned a moderate amount of grammar study and practice at home using the auxiliary course text; only that a demand for active mastery should not accompany the assignment. Deliberate exposure to a comprehensive range of grammatical forms and structures can definitely be a good thing. As such, grammar can be integrated into comprehension, reading and writing skills as long as it is de-emphasized in communicative classroom activities.

Once imbued with the ability to speak the target language, students will naturally progress towards correct grammatical usage

Reader's Reflection

Do you have ideas to increase grammar awareness without tapping into the conscious mind?

The JoF Approach to Homework

The role of homework is an emotionally charged issue for many teachers, as well as students. As teachers we are aware of how much there is to master when studying a second language, and we easily despair at the thought of doing it all in class. It might seem that students ought to perform part of the learning at home or in the language laboratory. As reasonable as this may sound, homework can, in fact, play a more negative role than positive in the acquisition process.

Most homework environments, both physically and psychological, are not compatible with an approach which focuses on acquisition. For most students, homework is associated with exercises and drills. The same is true of most language lab experiences. Thus, an approach such as JoF, which goes to great lengths to establish an optimal climate for acquisition, is very careful in suggesting and structuring work outside of class.

The skillful teacher, using the appropriate suggestive means and the rich resources provided by the group, fosters an excellent environment for acquisition within the classroom setting. Outside that environment, however, especially in the early stages, the climate may be very unfavorable. For many students their home study environment is an impoverished one and can be counter-productive. Great care must be exercised to ensure that the positive student attitudes being so carefully nurtured in the classroom are not undermined through needless mechanical and boring work at home.

Traditionally, homework tends to make the student focus on conscious activities about the language. As many of us know first hand, when we try to master the immense complexity of a language consciously, we can easily get discouraged. Conscious acquisition is virtually impossible because language rules operate at an unconscious level in natural ways. Since, the early stages of brain-compatible learning focus on developing a broad and deep base of comprehension out of which production can naturally emerge, written homework is risky. As it requires a substantially more complex level of competence than can be expected naturally, it will likely de-motivate and confuse the student rather than help.

There are, however, useful activities which students can engage in outside of class which will support the acquisition goals. A primary activity is listening. Most students own or have access to portable audio-cassette players, often with headphones. If they do not, then the language laboratory can be used. Listening activities using one's own personal cassette player are, in my experience, generally welcomed by students. And if the taped materials provide engaging, comprehensible input, motivation will remain high, and the acquisition process will be genuinely furthered. For instance, I provide my students

Most homework environments, both physically & psychologically, are not compatible with an approach which focuses on acquisition

with tapes of the second musical concert readings of the basic brain-based text we use. In addition, I also tape other texts and variations on them giving attention to authenticity of intonation and expression.

Some writing activities done at home, in moderation, can also be useful. I sometimes ask students to transcribe short sentences or paragraphs from tape listening. This activity connects a visual to auditory comprehension, and for some can serve to sharpen their auditory acuity. Or students can be given a written text with key words missing which they are asked to complete. However, in the early stages it is important that the missing words not require grammatical manipulation so choosing nouns for the blank spaces is appropriate. This activity stimulates the student's sense of contextual understanding rather than asking for a conscious capacity to manipulate grammatical forms. The latter may become a positive reinforcer later on.

Reader's Reflection

What kinds of activities might you assign for outside class learning?

Also I regularly suggest to students to read over the dramatic and/or dialogue texts lightly - as one would an interesting magazine article - just before going to sleep. This reading is to be accompanied by the passive second concert presentation of the same material recorded on cassette and furnished for their personal use. As the brain's conscious functioning begins to relax its control, an anchoring effect can occur in the more receptive mind.

Conscious learning tasks do, however, become increasingly appropriate later in the course as the skills of reading and writing receive greater attention. Conscious skill-learning is then useful if there is time to apply such skills. Somewhere after 25 to 30 hours of focusing on listening and oral skills, student motivation and interest is usually high enough to sustain some conscious attention on language mechanics, grammar and syntax. However, I still take care to avoid suggesting a traditional learning orientation.

Although the brain-compatible approach relies relatively less than other methods on student efforts outside of class, some students will want homework. Many students derive desired security from being able to expend large amounts of effort alone to master assigned tasks. I explain to students that they will have optimum success as they learn to tap their vast unconscious resources and relax their conscious controls. This can be a threatening prospect for certain students who need encouragement and affirming support in order to trust capacities they are unaware are present. Their rapid gains in acquisition skills during the first weeks, however, usually present enough concrete evidence to overcome initial doubts.

Conclusion

With most of the JoF teacher's attention being focused on providing a positively charged and enriched environment using the approach recommended in this book, Joyful Fluency will be the result your students naturally achieve. This approach which simply emphasizes the means, rather than the end, ironically produces guaranteed results. Now that you have digested the strategies outlined in the previous chapters, you will certainly need to give yourself time to implement them in your own work.

Essential in all ways to this process is that you remain in an optimal learning state yourself - relaxed, open, curious and expectant of success. You have nothing to lose as you experiment with brain-compatible approaches to learning, and everything to gain. As naturally as you learned to speak your native tongue, you will gain mastery joyfully as you proceed down the lane of brain-compatible teaching. Why be content with rote memorization techniques with students who are bored and withdrawn when you know that everyone (including yourself) can enjoy the language acquisition classroom and learn at an optimum level simultaneously? *You are about to transform your classroom and make a positively immeasurable impact on many... Congratulations!*

Great care must be exercised to ensure that the positive student attitudes being so carefully nurtured in the classroom are not undermined through needless mechanical and boring work at home

Introspection

What are my own feelings about the topics presented in this chapter? Why do I believe the way I do?

_____

_____

_____

_____

_____

Insights

What are some things I'm discovering now? What's the big picture?

_____

_____

_____

_____

_____

Practical Suggestions

What are the resulting actions that follow from my beliefs? In what ways might I improve?

_____

_____

_____

_____

Bibliography

Assagioli, Roberto (1965) *Psychosynthesis*, New York, NY: Viking Press.

Assagioli, R. (1973) *The Act of Will*, Baltimore, MD: Penguin.

Asher, James (1988) *Brainswitching: A Skill for the 21st Century*, Los Gatos, CA: Sky Oaks Productions.

Asher, J. (1986) *Learning Another Language Through Actions*. Expanded Third Edition, Los Gatos, CA: Sky Oaks Productions.

Asher, J. "The Strategy of Total Physical Response: An Application To Learning Russian", *International Review of Applied Linguistics*, 3: pp. 292-9.

Asher, J. "The Total Physical Response Approach to Second Language Learning", *Modern Language Journal*, 53: pp. 3-18.

Asher, J. and Kusudo, J. and de la Torre, R. "Learning a Second Language Through Commands: The Second Field Test", *Modern Language Journal*. 58:102, pp. 24-32.

Begley, Sharon, (1996) "Your Child's Brain", *Newsweek*, Feb. 19, pp. 57-61.

Condon, William, (1982) "Cultural Microrythms", *Interaction Rhythms*, pp.53-77.

Dhority, Lynn, (1991) *The ACT Approach: The Use of Suggestion for Integrative Learning*, PLS Verlag GmbH, An der Weide 27-28, 2800 Bremen, West Germany.

Dunn, Rita and Dunn, Kenneth (1978). *Teaching Students Through Their Individual Learning Styles: A Practical Approach*. Reston, VA: Reston Publishing Co.

Dunn, R. and Dunn, K. (1987). Dispelling Outmoded Beliefs About Student Learning. *Educational Leadership*, 44.6, pp. 55-61.

Dunn, K. and Dunn, R. (1992) *Bringing Out The Giftedness In Your Child*, New York, NY: John Wiley.

Fidelman, Carolyn, Multi-year grant, "In the French Body", FIPSE.

Gordon, David (1978) *Therapeutic Metaphors*, Cupertino, CA: Meta Publications.

Gordon, D. and Anderson, M. (1982) *Phoenix, Therapeutic Patterns of Milton H. Erickson*.

Jung, Carl (1964) *Man and His Symbols*, Garden City, NY: Doubleday.

Krashen, Stephen (1982) *Principles and Practice in Second Language Acquisition*, New York, NY: Pergamon Press.

Krashen, S. and Terrell, T. (1983) *The Natural Approach*, Alemany Press, P.O. Box 5265, San Francisco, CA 94101.

Lozanov, Georgi (1988) *Foreign Language Teacher's Manual*. New York, NY: Gordon and Breach Publishing.

Lozanov, G. (1979) *Suggestology and Outlines of Suggestopedia*, New York, NY: Gordon and Breach Publishing.

Lozanov, G. (1978) *Suggestology and Suggestopedia, Theory and Practice*, UNESCO Report ED - 78/WS/119.

Lozanov, G. and Balevski, P. (1975) "The Effect of the Suggestopedic System of Instruction on the Physical Development, State of Health, and Working Capacity of First and Second Grade Pupils." *Suggestology and Suggestopedia*, 1:3.

Lozanov, G. (1975) "Suggestopedia in Primary Schools", *Suggestology and Suggestopedia Journal*, 1:3.

Lozanov, G. (1975) "The Nature and History of the Suggestopedic System of Teaching Foreign Languages and its Experimental Prospects", *Suggestology and Suggestopedia Journal*, 1:1.

Ostrander, Sheila and Schroeder, Lynn (1979) *Superlearning*, New York, NY: Delacorte Press.

Rosenthal, Robert and Jacobson, L. (1968) *Pygmalion in the Classroom*, New York, NY: Holt, Rinehart and Winston.

Rosenthal, R. (1975) "The Pygmalion Effect Lives", *Psychology Today* 7:4, pp. 56-63.

Springer, Sally; Deutsch, Georg (1981) *Left Brain, Right Brain*, New York, NY: W.H. Freeman.

Terrell, Tracy "A Natural Approach to the Acquisition and Learning of a Language", *Modern Language Journal*, 61: pp. 325-336.

Terrell, T. "The Natural Approach to Language Teaching: An Update", *Modern Language Journal*, 66: pp. 121-131.

Wylie, Lawrence (1985) "Language Learning and Communication" *The French Review*, Vol. LVIII, No. 6, May, pp.777-785.

Trainings:

Learning Brain Expo®—An Amazing, 3-Day Professional Development Event. Join top neuroscientists and education experts as they present the most recent findings in brain research and translate them into powerful new paradigms for teaching to enhance learning, foster student development and raise achievement. For complete conference details and to register, visit www.brainexpo.com or call 800-325-4769. Outside the U. S., call 858-546-7555.

6-day In-depth Training on Brain-Compatible Learning—Offered in numerous U.S. cities including: San Diego, CA; San Antonio, TX and Boston, Mass. Dozens of critical insights and hundreds of strategies about the brain and how to enhance learning. (888) 638-7246

5-day Facilitator Training—Blending current brain research with presentation and persuasion skills. (888) 638-7246

Ongoing Transformational Learning Seminars—Focusing on the Dialogue Process for organizations, businesses and individuals. Contact Freeman Dhority, 1990 Vassar Drive, Boulder, CO, 80305. Email: fdhority@aol.com.

Books & Other Resources:

For a **FREE** catalog of brain-compatible learning resources, call The Brain Store® at (800) 325-4769 or (858) 546-7555. Or, visit www.thebrainstore.com and browse the online catalog.

Brain and Language: A Journal of Clinical, Experimental, and Theoretical Research, by Harry Whitaker, Ph.D, Editor (Published monthly by Elsevier)

Tools for Engagement: Managing Emotional States for Learner Success, by Eric Jensen (2003, The Brain Store®)

Healing Words, by Larry Dossey, M.D. (1993, Harper San Francisco)

Innovative Approaches to Language Teaching, by Robert W. Blair, Editor (1982, Heinle & Heinle Publishers, Boston, Mass.)

The Language Instinct, by Steven Pinker (1995, Harper Perennial, New York)

Index

Lynn Freeman Dhority received his Ph.D. in Languages and Literature from Harvard University where he was awarded the Boylston Prize for Outstanding Teaching. He studied personally with Dr. Georgi Lozanov in the art of suggestive-accelerative teaching (Suggestopedia) and became an international leader in holistic learning and teaching with his book, *The ACT Approach: The Use of Suggestion for Integrative Learning*. He taught German for over twenty years at the University of Massachusetts in Boston where he established the holistic, integrative approach to teaching languages described in *Joyful Fluency*. His extensive background includes years of experience in psychology and counseling skills, organizational learning and collective dialogue. He is currently a consultant to organizations internationally for transformational learning and lives with his wife in Boulder, Colorado where he co-directs the Boulder Learning Series.

Eric Jensen, former teacher and adjunct faculty at the University of California at San Diego, National University, and the University of San Diego is the author of best-selling *Student Success Secrets, The Little Book of Big Motivation, Brain-Based Learning, B's and A's in 30 Days, Different Brains Different Learners, SuperTeaching, Tools for Engagement*, and *Introduction To Brain Compatible Learning*. He was the co-founder of SuperCamp, the nation's first and largest brain-compatible learning program for teens. Currently Jensen conducts trainings for schools, organizations, and Fortune 500 companies worldwide. He was a key contributor to the implementation of Australia's and New Zealand's learning revolution which trained over 5,000 teachers in the brain-based approach. Trainers from AT&T, Disney, IBM, GTE, Hewlett-Packard, Motorola, Altantic Bell and three branches of the military have used his methods. Jensen is listed in "Who's Who Worldwide" and is a former Outstanding Young Man of America selection. He remains deeply committed to making a positive, significant and lasting difference in the way the world learns.

The Brain Store® encourages your feedback on our products. If you would like to assist us, please mail or fax your correspondence to the address/fax number below. Thank you!

The Brain Store®
4202 Sorrento Valley Blvd., Ste B, San Diego, CA 92121
Phone: 858-546-7555 or Fax: 858-546-7560
www.thebrainstore.com
E-Mail: info@thebrainstore.com